How to Start, Run & Grow a Successful T-Shirt Business

Work from Home- Print and Sell Shirts Online and Offline

A Great Passive Income Business Model

CW00952100

By

Richard Finley

Autumn Leaf
PUBLISHING HOUSE

Design & Illustration by Robin Wright

First Edition

Contents

Introduction – Who am I? 4

Why You Might Care 6

Why T-Shirts? 8

What You'll Learn From Me 9

Failure Doesn't Have to Be an Option 11

How to Get the Most Out of This Book 12

How to Create Your Own Product: Part One, Making the Shirts Yourself 15

Bleach Stencil Design T-Shirts 16

The Supplies 17

Stencils? 18

Choosing a Spray Bottle 19

Prep Yourself 20

Placing Your Image 20

Getting On With It 21

Let it Be 23

The Downside to Bleach Designed Shirts 23

Stencils + Fabric Ink 24

The Supplies 24

The Stencil...25

Attach the Stencil...26

Pep The Ink and Do It..26

Dry and Cure 27

The Downside to Fabric Ink and Rollers 28

Screen Printing at Home **28**

The Supplies 29

Choosing Your Design + Printing It.........................30

Get Your Frame 31

What is Photo Emulsion, and Do I Need It? 32

Get Dark 33

Once We've Dried... 34

Exposing Your Screen 35

And... Leave It! 37

Wash It Off 38

Actually Making a Shirt 39

If That Sounded Like a Lot of Work... 41

The Downside to Screen Printing at Home 42

Vinyl Graphics at Home..**42**

Supplies 43

The Steps...43

Set Your Design 44

Set It 44

Pull it Off 45

The Downsides of Vinyl Shirts 46

How to Create Your Own Product, Part Two: Companies That Handle Printing and Inventory For You 47

Spreadshop...48

CafePress 50

Zazzle 50

RedBubble 51

Amazon Merch 52

Shopify + Amazon Works 54

Minor Things You'll Need.......................................59

What About Shipping? 60

How to Create Your Designs....................................62

You Can Also Outsource..64

What is a Target Audience, and Do I Need One? 66

What's Your Niche? 69

Underserved Niches are Best 70

Using Amazon to Find Your Niches...........................71

What is a Brand? Do I Need One? 75

Selling Online: The Ins, The Outs, The Important Things............81

How To Really Sell Your Product – Mock-ups 82

Etsy..84

Selling on Facebook Marketplace....................................86

Another Option: Selling at Local Events 87

Creating Your Own Website..89

How to Sell on Your Website 91

What About Taking Payment? 93

What is a Business Plan, and Do I Need One?...........................95

The Backbone of a Good Business Plan 97

Using the SMART Goals System 98

What a Specific Goal Means...99

What a Measurable Goal Means...100

What an Achievable Goal Means 101

What a Relevant Goal Means..101

What a Time-Bound Goal Means 102

Every Goal, Use This System 103

What Else Do You Need With a Business Plan?..................103

Elements of a Traditional Business Plan 104

Examples of Excellent, Short, To-The-Point Mission

Statements 105

6

Back to your Business Plan... a Company Description 107

Market Analysis...107

Organization, Management, and Business Structure..........108

Your Product Line...109

Marketing Plans 109

Finance Requests? Put Them Here 109

Financial Projections 110

Appendix 111

The Other Side of Business Plans: Short and Sweet.............112

Bottom Line on Business Plans..114

The Nitty Gritty: Bank Accounts, LLC, Taxes, and More Boring
Things You Need to Know About...116

Choosing a Business Name..117

Why an LLC is For You 119

How to Handle Taxes 122

Business Taxes and Other Things You Can't Avoid...............124

Other Things to Keep in Mind When Starting Your Business 125

Let's Talk Banking 126

Account, Receipts, and Other Boring Things........................128

What is a Tax Deduction? What Can I Deduct? 130

Why Do I Need to Pay Self-Employment Taxes? 131

Gross Receipt Tax VS State Income Tax 133

Should I Do My Taxes Myself?! 134

The Michael Scott Lesson in Proper Pricing 136

What We Learn From This...137

There Are Like 800 Things to Consider in Pricing 138

So How Much Profit? 140

Where Does Wholesale Fit in? 143

What Can I Expect to Pay Upfront? 144

Do I Need Cushion: A Lesson 150

Should You Get Investor Funding? 151

What About SBA-Guarantee?...153

Be Careful of Giving Up *Too* Much.....................................156

Expanding 101: Opening a Storefront, Hiring Help, and
Expanding Your Product Line 158

The Cost Involved 159

Finding The Perfect Spot 162

A Mall/Shopping Plaza Versus a Downtown Location Versus
Standalone 166

A Mall, or a Shopping Center 166

A Downtown Location...168

A Standalone Storefront 169

When To Hire Help..170

Expanding Your Product Line: Be Careful............................174

Social Media, Marketing, and How to Gain + Keep Customers 177

Do I Have To?..178

Why You Need Social Media 179

How Often Should I Be Posting?...180

Don't Ignore Them, Though 181

What Do I Even Post?! 182

Be Sure Your Social Media Matches Your Brand.................183

Facebook Advertising...184

What Posts Do Best?..185

Facebook Data 186

You Can Also Use Outside Platforms 187

Mobile Matters..187

Instagram Ads..188

#Hashtag 190

Do I Need TikTok?..192

Notes for Best Social Media Ad Practices 195

Connecting Your Social Media Accounts..............................196

Running Google Ads...197

Other Marketing Options...199

Speaking of Sales..201

Put It All Together, Now *204*

Introduction – Who am I?

After the 20th person asked me how I started my business, what made me choose this business, and how I was able to be *so* stinking successful (not a brag!), I decided that it was easier to simply *write a book* about it rather than sit talking business at parties or events.

You see, I sell t-shirts. That seems boring, I know, but it's true. I started as a teen screen printing at home as a hobby, mostly. I wanted fun, funny, or different t-shirts, but I wasn't willing to spend $30+ on a single shirt, even if I could find a design I liked. You know how teens are so edgy. I thought I was the funniest person ever.

It turns out, other people also thought I was funny.

I started making t-shirts for friends at school, for birthdays or holidays, and then for family events. It got to the point where friends of friends asked for t-shirts, some custom, some designs I already had.

I had *no idea* what I was doing, building what would end up being a very successful business. I just knew I liked to create, and I was doing something no one else in the area was doing.

I started selling my shirts online, and it turns out... a lot of people outside of my friend group thought I was funny, too.

I quit my dead-end job without thinking too hard about the consequences (ah, to be young) and threw myself into building my business from the ground up. I had no marketing degree, no business degree, *no idea* what I was doing or how to get it done. But I pulled myself together; I took a ton of books out of the local library and made some pretty serious mistakes at one point. My family still won't let me forget the time my cat dumped fabric ink all over the carpet.

Now, I have a successful online shop. I have a small storefront where I sell t-shirts that are more locally focused and have partnered with numerous local and national businesses, nonprofits, and teams to create custom t-shirts, tote bags, and sweaters. I'm a lot older than when I first started, a whole lot wiser, and I still think I'm hilarious. Some things never change, I suppose.

Why You Might Care

I'm not telling you this to brag. Instead, I'm telling you this to help you understand. *I know what I'm doing.* I've started a business from the ground up. I've stayed up late online researching tax laws and if my brand new desk is tax-deductible or not (it is!).

I have cried after screwing up a few dozen shirts and had to toss the whole batch.

I have been exactly where you have, thinking about starting a new business and doing something I actually enjoy, without being under the thumb of an idiot boss who doesn't know what he is doing or working for an awful company that doesn't care about me.

I wrote this book not just to avoid those annoying conversations about what I do and how I started, but to help people who were *just like me* at one point, hoping to start something amazing and give themselves and their families a better life.

It doesn't matter your business experience or if you even have any. It doesn't matter if you don't know how to set up a website or if you know the difference between PayPal and Square for taking payment. It doesn't matter if you've never run a marketing campaign on social media or if that is your full-time job.

You can build this business, and you can be successful. I truly believe that.

Why T-Shirts?

This might be the most common question I get. *Why t-shirts? Why not mugs or hats or bags or...?* You get the point.

To their credit, I have expanded since I first started so many years ago. I don't just make t-shirts; I also do sweaters, totes bags, and even some casual dresses on occasion. I've been known to dip my toe into fanny packs (they're coming back, y'all), hoodies, and even mugs. However, t-shirts always have been and always will be the bread and butter of my business.

Why?

Because t-shirts are *great*. The cost to get into creating your own t-shirts is pretty low. When buying in bulk, good-quality shirts are not that expensive, especially when you consider how much they sell for retail.

Learning to create your own designs is an experience in creativity and one that I personally love. If you want to express yourself, your clothing is often the first place to do it.

Clothing is also one of those things *we all need*. Unlike businesses that sell products that are not strictly necessary or needed, everyone needs something to wear. Do they need your custom designs? Maybe not need – but if they are going to buy clothes anyway, they probably will buy something they enjoy.

In short? T-shirts are easy to get started with, fun to design and create, and everyone needs one. When you look at it like that, why *wouldn't* you get started with t-shirts?!

What You'll Learn From Me

I have tried my hardest to create the most comprehensive guide to making t-shirts, selling t-shirts, and building a business from the ground up. This is truly the only book that you need to get your journey started.

I wasn't initially going to write this book. I actually bought *several* similar books on Amazon to try and find something to offer folks who wanted to learn more about what I did. However, they were all... not great. Well, they ranged from *really awful* to *just fine.* So few of them covered things that I, as a business owner, felt were vitally important. Was it because these people had never run a business themselves? Maybe. Maybe they were just so close to the process that they didn't know what some people didn't know. After you have been doing something for so long, after all, you sort of become desensitized to the finer aspects of it.

I wanted this to be as comprehensive as possible, and I have tried to write it in a way that anyone can understand. I've broken down difficult topics, I've taken a tone that *should* read as if I was speaking to you over lunch, and I've left no stone of my own business unturned. You get the real, inside look at how I started my own business and what you need to do to start yours, too.

That said, this isn't going to be *easy.* So few things in life worth doing are, though. Think of this as a cheat code to get your business off the ground. You can avoid some of the major mistakes so many folks make and get a leg up. However, it's up to you to put in the work and make it successful.

Failure Doesn't Have to Be an Option

Scary statistics incoming: according to the Bureau of Labor Statistics Business Employment Data, approximately 20% of small businesses will fail within the first year of being open.

30% fail within the first two years.

A shocking 50% of small businesses fail within the first 5 years.

If you make it past 5 years, you're not out of the woods. **70%** of small businesses fail by year 10. That is... scary, and you might be asking yourself why I'm telling you these scary statistics. It's certainly not because I want you to fail, because I don't! I want you to find success. It's because I want you to *take this seriously* and really listen to what I have to say.

I made it; I'm part of that 30% that has not just survived but thrived year after year, even through the economic downturn and some bonehead mistakes. Not everyone gets that chance. I don't believe I was 'lucky' to survive, despite what some people tell me. Instead, I think I was smart.

I can teach you how to be smart, too.

I don't want you to be one of those statistics. If you go at it without this book, if you just skim the basics and 'wing it,' or if you just throw something together and hope for the best, however, I can't promise you success. I can promise you if you take the time to read what I have to share, you take your new business venture seriously, and you follow the steps I've laid out (even the boring ones, like a business plan and tax information), you're going to have the best chance at beating the odds and being successful.

You *can* do this.

How to Get the Most Out of This Book

If you're reading this, we have already established you're interested in starting your own business, and creating t-shirts is where you want to go. That's awesome! Before you rush off, I do have a recommendation on how to get the most out of this book.

When you sit down to read, I recommend you have a notebook with you, a Word document up on your PC, or even Google Docs open on your phone. When I say something that speaks to you, or you read something that gives you inspiration, you should jot that down for later. Don't trust yourself to remember it – this is a dense book with a lot of information. You may forget that brilliant idea or helpful hint once you've moved onto the next chapter.

There are also a few sections in here where I ask you to brainstorm things for your business plan, your business's *future*, and more. This can be written down in your book, and you can easily reference it when you need to.

You also may have to read a chapter more than once. That's totally okay! As you move along in your business creation and steps, you may find that coming back to the marketing section, or getting information on creating an LLC, is helpful. That is what this book is for.

I've created this as a comprehensive, one-stop shop for you. With just this book, some drive, and a sprinkle of hard work, you can get your own business off the ground and start selling your product nearly immediately, which is pretty exciting.

Are you ready to get started?

(Sidenote: Would you please consider leaving a review where you purchased this book online? I plan on actually reading customer reviews so that I can improve my next book project. Thanks in advance!)

How to Create Your Own Product: Part One, Making the Shirts Yourself

Believe it or not, creating your shirts by hand is *not* the most common way people start their business.

Dropshipping and third-party creators are all real, viable options in this business, and I'm going to get into that in a minute.

However, if you want to physically create your own shirts from the blank canvas up and manage your inventory, I've got you covered. As previously mentioned, this was how I started, and it's still how many of my designs are created. I think there is something fun and raw about handling your own product and having that full level of control. It's okay if it's not for you, but I've got instructions on how to make the most common design types if you do decide to go this route!

Bleach Stencil Design T-Shirts

This is such a fun way to design t-shirts, and it can create a really wonderful, unique finished product. No two t-shirts are quite the same when done this way, and that's really the appeal!

Doing your own bleached t-shirt designs isn't difficult once you get the hang of it, and you can produce multiple t-shirts in one sitting without too much hassle. When you're considering the best designs for your bleached shirts, be sure to think about the color contrast of the shirts to the bleach and the way you can use negative space.

You need a handful of supplies to make these t-shirts a reality, but these are actually things you can easily pick up at nearly any store. This is one of the big benefits of doing bleached shirts – you need almost zero specialty equipment or tools.

The Supplies

Colored t-shirt of your choice

Small spray bottle

Household bleach

A large piece of cardboard

Paper towels

Stencils of your choice

Stencils?

In order to transfer your desired design to the shirt, you're going to need a stencil. There are a few ways you can handle this. You can absolutely just go to your local craft store and pick up the stencils you want to use, but this doesn't have a lot of customization for you. You'll be using simply what they have to offer.

You can make your own stencils fairly easily. If you have a Cricut machine, or another vinyl cutting machine, printing off custom stencils is as easy as a few mouse clicks. No matter how you feel about the morals of the company and the direction they are going, this is a very easy way to get custom stencils quickly. If you're using a Cricut, be sure to use just regular vinyl, just like you would put on a sign. This holds up best to the bleach!

You can also cut out your own stencils, though it will obviously be more work. Print your desired image on cardstock, or have it printed at a print shop. Using an Exacto knife and a steady hand, you can cut out the design. Make sure you have sharp, accurate lines because otherwise, it will really show up in the final product.

The smaller and simpler your design is, the easier it is going to be to cut out yourself – just keep this in mind!

Choosing a Spray Bottle

Picking the right spray bottle is important! Depending on how you want the design to look, a bottle with a fine mist *or* a big, splotchy spray can work well. If you have never done bleach t-shirts before yourself, I recommend buying several different nozzles and experimenting on scrap fabric or t-shirts to see what spray pattern you like best.

If you want to be exceptionally organized, you can do test shirts for each spray bottle you try and keep the test spray with the bottle labeled properly. That way, if you decide you want to do another style of shirt, you don't have to guess which bottle of bleach is best – just grab and go!

Prep Yourself

Take your spray bottle and fill it up halfway with water. Fill the remaining half with bleach, and shake well. Your goal is to change the color of the shirt, not eat through it all the way – diluting the bleach will get you to this point.

While you can use a more intense bleach solution, doing a 1-1 ratio is fairly standard and will give you the best results with relatively minimal risks.

Placing Your Image

Once you've got your stencil, cut out, and your bleach solution prepped, lay out your t-shirt. Put your piece of cardboard *between* the front and the back of the shirt to protect the back from the bleach.

Place your image carefully on your shirt. If you're using vinyl, you can peel it off and carefully place it. Be sure your placement is exactly where you want it before you stick it on the shirt because there is no coming back. If you cut your design out, I recommend using an adhesive to stick it onto the shirt – a simple glue stick, like you would find in a kindergartener's backpack, works fairly well without leaving a huge amount of mess or residue.

Be sure to **press firmly** against the design to ensure even sticking. You don't want any air bubbles or loose edges where bleach can sneak in and hurt your design.

Getting On With It

Your stencil is set, and you have your bleach solution prepared – it's time to do it!

Without sounding too obvious, bleach is a chemical, and you should be careful with it! Be sure to do all of your production in a well-ventilated area. Outdoors is technically best, but that can be a struggle with the wind and the elements – also, some of us simply don't live somewhere that you can do production outside year around. A garage with the doors up is usually a great compromise, but ventilation is incredibly important.

Be sure there is nothing important around your work area that might get damaged by any stray bleach sprays!

Once you're situated, it's time to start spraying the bleach. Start with the inside of the design and work outwards, which will help prevent you from over-spraying too much.

The color should start changing immediately. I cannot stress this enough: do not oversaturate your shirt!

If you put too much on, the bleach can leak under the stencil and cause some serious bleeding, hurting the final product. It can also bleed through the cardboard to the back of the shirt, which obviously doesn't provide the desired results.

Spray slowly and carefully – it will continue to lighten as time passes! The slower and more careful you are, the better the final product will be.

Once you've applied the amount the bleach you need, use your paper towels to blot the excess off of your stencil. If you don't, it can collect in little bleach puddles and ruin your design.

Let it Be

Your bleach is on, so let it sit until it dries completely. Removing the stencil and the cardboard interior can end up ruining the design, and the shirt, if there is still wet bleach.

Once the shirt is dry to the touch, remove the cardboard and the stencil. Wash to remove excess bleach, and you're done!

The Downside to Bleach Designed Shirts

These shirts are really fun and can create some incredibly unique designs. They also tend to appeal to a *type* of market, those who value creativity, quirkiness, etc. However, it's difficult to scale up the production of bleach shirts. While each t-shirt doesn't take that much time individually, setting up each shirt and then letting it dry can be time-consuming. This method definitely needs space to do properly.

If this doesn't bother you, though, and your target market finds bleached t-shirts appealing, this could be an excellent process for you.

Stencils + Fabric Ink

Another popular way of creating t-shirts with a design is using stencils, a roller, and fabric ink to essentially print your own shirts. Like the bleach methods, this requires a little precision and some focus, but once you get the process down, it's easy to do!

The Supplies

A sheet of clear acetate or transparency film

X-Acto knife

Masking tape or another form of adhesive for the stencil

Fabric ink of any color

A painting tray or a paper plate

A mini foam paint roller

A t-shirt of any color

A pillowcase

An iron

The Stencil

Just like with the bleach method, you could use a stencil from a craft store or a sheet of acetate to create your own. If you are creating your own, print out your desired design, and set it under the sheet of acetate. You can tape the paper to the acetate to help keep it stable.

Using your X-Acto knife, carefully cut out your stencil. It's very important to get sharp, precise lines – any imperfections will show up. You can also use a Cricut machine to cut out vinyl stencils if you have one.

Warning: This method of cutting out your design and using fabric ink to roll the print on doesn't translate well for letters or words. Unless you've used a Cricut stencil you have printed, the words can be very blocky and look more like a stamped final product. Just keep that in mind when you're choosing your designs!

Attach the Stencil

Now that you've got your stencil prepped attach the stencil to your shirt. You can use masking tape in the corners, or you can even use a spray adhesive and spray down the whole backside of the stencil before laying it out. You want to make sure that your stencil is as close to the shirt as possible to help prevent bleeding.

Pep The Ink and Do It

Pour your fabric ink into a roller tray or a small plate. Something to keep in mind is that water-based ink doesn't always work well with darker fabrics, so be sure you do some experiments – white ink really doesn't take well to a black shirt, in general.

You can use any size foam roller you want, but I personally prefer a smaller roller. I find that a smaller roller both uses less ink, which is nice and gives me better control over the final product. A larger roller is faster but wasteful.

Roll your roller in the ink several times to saturate it before carefully rolling it across the stencil. Find the right balance of pressure – pushing too hard is going to cause the ink the bleed under the stencil, while not pushing hard enough is going to leave splotches and light spots.

Peel your stencil off to see the final product! This is the time to touch up any areas you may have missed or messed up.

Dry and Cure

You're not done! There are a few extra steps, depending on your fabric ink choice. Be sure to read the instructions, but generally, you need to dry and then heat the shirt to get to the final product.

Let the shirt air dry completely. Once all the ink is dry, not tacky, plug in your iron. Covering the design with a pillowcase to prevent ironing directly on the ink, you want to slowly and carefully iron the design. Be sure to heat it up completely and get all of the edges.

Once you've ironed your design completely, your ink should be set! The heat helps the ink bond to the fabric properly, so it won't simply wash out when you toss it in the washer.

The Downside to Fabric Ink and Rollers

This is a great method to get a very specific look to a shirt without a lot of supplies. However, this method has its drawbacks, just like any other.

Just like with bleaching, how many shirts you produce is limited by the room you have. Most people doing these at home can only roll 5-10 shirts at a time before pausing to let everything dry. If you are only selling a few shirts a day, this probably isn't really a concern, but as you hopefully grow your business, it can become difficult to keep up.

Screen Printing at Home

You don't have to outsource your screen printing if you really love the look of a screen-printed t-shirt. This is actually a process you can do at home, though it is slightly more involved than our previous processes. This is also how I started! When done right, screen printing can look very professional.

The Supplies

A screen for screen printing (see below for details)

150-watt lightbulb

Photo emulsion

Squeegee for screen printing

Fabric paint

2 pieces of glass

Printer

X-Acto knife

Pillowcase

Iron

Choosing Your Design + Printing It

When thinking about your design, simpler is going to be easier when you first start. Look for something relatively solid to get the process down.

You're going to want to print out your design on dark paper or filled in with black ink. Using your X-Acto knife, carefully cut out your design. Just like with other designs, sharp edges are so important! You should be left with a solid image in black.

To test if your design will work, hold it up to the light after you cut it out. If you can see light through it, your paper isn't dark enough. You can double up on dark paper, or you can literally just color the other side with a marker to get that thicker, deeper color.

When you get into detailed images, I recommend you using transparency paper. This is easy to find online or at craft stores near you.

Get Your Frame

Okay, so you're going to need a screen printing frame in order to, well, screen print. Makes sense, right? There are a few ways you can get one.

One is to simply buy a frame online. Amazon has them, as well as specialty online shops like ScreenPrinting.com. For each design you are going to do, you're going to need a new screen. This seems like a big investment, but if you're going to do a limited amount of designs, this isn't going to be an awful expense.

You can also build your own frames if you are handy and have extra time. Take a square wood frame and a staple gun, and stretch something called "110 polyester mesh". This is something specifically designed for screen printing and pushing ink through. You can get a few yards for $10 or so on Amazon, depending on the seller.

You don't need to create a perfect frame, just something solid enough that it won't warp and sits flat. You're going to want the right tension in the fabric – it should be tight enough to be taut and sturdy, but not so tight it rips from the staples. A regular staple gun is all you need, but be sure all of the staples lay flat. You don't want your frame to wobble.

Then, take painter's tape and tape the inside and the outside edges where the fabric meets the frame. This helps prevent any dripping or bleeding.

If you've never made one before, but you like the idea, I recommend ordering one just to see what it looks like, what the tension is like, etc. It just gives you a good idea of what you're going for. You can also go to a local craft supply store that carries them and just pick one up and handle it.

What is Photo Emulsion, and Do I Need It?

Yes, you absolutely need photo emulsion! This is key to, well, screen printing! You can buy photo emulsion formula in many craft stores or online, and it normally comes in two parts – the base formula and an additional liquid that is needed to activate it. Follow the instructions for your specific container, but most of the time, you just add one to the other and mix it up.

This product is really the core of screen printing, and it is a light-sensitive solution that basically burns the stencil *directly* into the fabric of the screen.

Get Dark

The hardest part of this process is getting darkness because you need an area of *pitch black* in order to get this to work. You can use a closet, but you need to make sure no light is getting into any cracks. A basement or attic can also work; as long as you have a very dark area, you can section off.

Once you've got your area darkened properly, it's time to prep your screen.

Note: This is how my own solution I prefer to use, Speedball brand, works. Be sure to read the instructions of your own brand very carefully, and if they deviate at all, follow the instructions on the package!

Apply a long, thin line of the solution at the top of the

fabric of your screen, and then using your squeegee, pull it down over the entire fabric. You want a very thin but even coat.

Once one side is coated, flip it over and do the same to the second. You need to work quickly before the solution has started to dry.

Once both sides of the fabric are coated, place the screen in your dark area. Store it horizontally, not vertically, so there is no drip or issue. You need to let this sit for anywhere from 1-3 hours, depending on your specific brand. You can use a very low-powered fan and cut the dry time in half – just make sure it's not too powerful, or it will move the wet product around.

Once We've Dried...

Once your solution is dried and ready, it's time to expose the image! You *do not* need a lightbox, no matter what you have read online or what someone swears. A 150-watt light bulb is enough to light; you don't need to invest in a lightbox.

Check your solution for the exact time you need to expose to light in order to get the result you want. There should also be details on how far away your light source needs to be – each solution is going to be a little different, so be sure to follow the instructions.

I use the 150-watt light bulb in a bare socket that hangs *over* my table, and I have sort of crafted a metal dome out of a tin pie plate to help fucus the light on the frame. You can buy metal lampshades and even specific lamps for this process, but as you're starting out, if you're looking to save money, a DIY solution is *totally* fine.

You also need something matte black to put the screen on for the exposure process. An old chalkboard works great, and you can usually find them pretty cheap second-hand. I bought one of those kid's easels from a thrift store and pulled it apart to get what I needed. You want it matte black, so it sucks up the light instead of reflecting it back onto the screen.

Exposing Your Screen

Lay your black matte surface down on the floor, and

situate your light, so it is over the top.

Place your dried screen face-down on top of the board. You want the non-recessed part facing *up* and towards you.

Take your cut-out stencil or black paper and lay it *in reverse* on top of your screen. For some designs, this doesn't matter, but if you're using words or direction-oriented pictures, take care.

Place a piece of very clean glass overtop of the image to hold it securely against the screen.

Note: Check out your local thrift store for frames! Picking up a relatively large glass frame is a great, cheap way to get a nice piece of glass for your use without breaking the bank. It's only really there to hold your design without moving while it is exposed, so as long as it is bigger than the screen, you're in good shape.

Once you've got your setup, double-check your *exact* specifications. For most of my images, I cure my screens for 35-40 minutes, with my light being 18-20 inches away from the screen. *Double-check* your photo emulsion for their exact directions, and follow that – each is a little different! Have I said that often enough yet?!

And... Leave It!

Once you've got, it set up, and your glass is situated where it needs to be, turn your light on *and leave it.* Seriously, set a timer and walk away. Don't touch it, don't fuss with it, don't even look at it funny.

If your solution says let cure for 35 minutes, just leave it there and let it cure. This is where many people end up screwing up their design. Once the light is turned on, and your screen is exposed, just leave it alone.

Come back once the time is up, and you can turn off the light and remove the stencil. It *should* darken around the areas that were exposed to light, while the area that was covered by the stencil will still be fresh and lighter.

Note: A lot of people fail their first time doing this, but if you follow my directions, you *shouldn't* fail. I have always followed these steps closely, and I have yet to ruin a screen. Be careful with accidental light exposure while your photo emulsion is drying, cure for the proper amount of time, and use glass to keep your stencil in place. If you do fail, don't be discouraged. Identify what went wrong, and try again.

Wash It Off

Once your stencil is set, the last step is to just wash it off. You are going to want to use *room temperature* water and a high-powered faucet. Some people use their outside hose, but mine is too cold and will damage it. I use my bathtub and haven't ever had an issue.

Keep spraying, and eventually, the photo emulsion will come off where the stencil was, leaving you with a design. Once you've gotten your design uncovered, you're set – you've made your first real screen, and you're ready.

Pro Tip: Hold your screen up to a light source. If you see any small pinholes where the photo emulsion *should* have filled, just cover those with painter's tape, so no accidental leaks happen!

Actually Making a Shirt

Alright! You've got your screen ready; it's time to actually *make* your shirt!

If this is your *very first-time* screen printing ever, I recommend using a few scrap shirts to test before actually doing the ones you want to sell. This way, you can gauge pressure and see how well your ink shows up.

Lay out your shirt on a flat surface. I like to work on a large piece of cardboard over a table, but you ideally want something relatively firm. Don't do it on a soft surface, like a couch or carpet. Be sure there are no wrinkles or folds, especially where you want your design.

Place your screen over the shirt so that the recessed side is facing *up*. You want the screen to be flat against the shirt. Place the screen so that the design is where you picture it on the shirt – that could be centered completely, more to the top (most common), to one side, etc.

Pro Tip: Your ink will dry a lot darker than it looks when wet! You can absolutely mix fabric ink colors to get the perfect shade, but remember it won't dry the same color it is wet.

Place a little 'puddle' or glug of ink at the top of the screen. Using your squeegee, drag the paint gently across the screen to cover your design. You are *not* pressing this into the shirt yet; you are just flooding the image and coating the screen with paint. You only want to go in one direction, whether that is top to bottom or bottom to top. Top to bottom is generally easier.

Now that the image is flooded, you can go back and press the fabric ink into the image using the squeegee. This is where knowledge and experience come in – if you press too hard, you risk the ink spreading. However, if you don't press enough, you risk the image getting splotchy or not dark enough.

Just like with flooding the image, you want to go in just one direction, top to bottom.

Once you have transferred your image onto your shirt, carefully remove the screen – it might stick a little bit to the shirt from the ink, but just be careful!

At this point, check your image. If you're happy with how much ink you have and how dark it is, you can hang it up and proceed to the next shirt. You can't re-print this, so you cannot fix the shirt you have done – however, you will know for next time.

Hang up your shirt until the image is dry. I use clothes pins, and a long line hung up in my workspace to give everything plenty of space.

Once it is dry, following the instructions on your specific brand of fabric ink, set your design. For most, you're going to want to lay the dry shirt out flat, cover it with a pillowcase to protect it from direct contact, and iron the design to set the ink. Once everything is set, you can wash the shirt, and you're good to go!

If That Sounded Like a Lot of Work...

I understand! Screen printing seems like a lot of work upfront. However, once you have your screens readied and prepared, the hard part is done! Actually, applying the ink on the shirt only takes a few minutes from start to finish, and it's *very* easy to set up an 'assembly line' of creating shirts where you can make money in an afternoon.

Once established, though, you don't need to remake your screens!

The Downside to Screen Printing at Home

As previously mentioned, it can be difficult to get started with screen printing, and many people struggle at first with setting up their screens. Each time you choose a new design, you need to create a new screen, which can be time-consuming if you want to offer many different styles and designs.

Vinyl Graphics at Home

Yes, you can absolutely do vinyl graphics at home! Vinyl graphics on shirts are a very specific look. They generally have a shiny, textured look and create a very 3D effect on the shirt. This isn't for every graphic, but it's very achievable to do yourself if this is the style that you want.

Supplies

Iron-on vinyl sheets + Cricut machine

X-Acto knife

Plain paper

Iron

The Steps

Gather your supplies and choose your design! The easiest way to do complex designs is using a Cricut machine with iron-on vinyl, but there are other iron-on vinyl supplies – you don't need to spend a lot of money on an expensive machine, especially at first.

If you go this route, you are going to want to print out your desired design and cut it out with a steady hand and your X-Acto knife.

You can draw on your vinyl to help guide your design, but be sure to draw on the shiny side of the paper. Vinyl iron-on paper has two sides – a matte side and a shiny side. The shiny side is going to be the side that peels away, so you can do whatever you want to it before that point.

Set Your Design

Once you have your vinyl cut and ready, no matter how you handled it, it's time to get your shirt prepped. Lay out your shirt on a heat-resistant surface, like an ironing board or a stack of towels.

Place your vinyl where you want it on the shirt shiny-side up. The matte side is going to go against the shirt because that is the side that will stick to it.

Set It

Place *something* over the vinyl to protect it from direct heat. The goal is gentle, steady heat, and if you put the iron on the vinyl directly, it can pucker up, creating lumps and an unappealing final product. I just use simple printer paper because it's a cheap solution that works really, really well.

My method is to put one sheet over the vinyl and touch the iron gently to the paper to set the vinyl graphic. After, I put a few more sheets on top to protect the graphic – I like using 5 total, which provides a good balance of protection.

Once your vinyl is protected completely, iron the vinyl for 15-20, checking after 10 seconds over the paper to fully set the design. If you have a very large design, I recommend doing it in sections to ensure your vinyl is set for each section.

Pull it Off

Once you've ironed the vinyl on, remove your protective paper barrier. Starting at one corner, gently peel the glossy top off to reveal the ironed-on vinyl graphic. If the full piece of vinyl is pulling away from the shirt, it is *not* properly secured, and you need to go back in with your iron and more heat.

Once the shiny top is removed, you're done. Really! Unlike our other methods of placing designs, vinyl shirts take the shortest time from start to finish. This is a huge plus, especially if you're processing many shirts at one time.

The Downsides of Vinyl Shirts

Vinyl has a very specific look. It's shiny and textured, and it isn't suitable for every design.

It also can be expensive to get into if you want to use a Cricut machine. If you don't, however, it can be difficult to make complex designs with any consistency. Sure, you can do one or two designs by hand – but if you're going to be *selling* these designs, hand-cutting dozens of designs can be incredibly laborious and time-consuming.

How to Create Your Own Product, Part Two: Companies That Handle Printing and Inventory For You

So you've got a design and an idea, but you *don't* want to invest a ton of money upfront, and you're not interested in storing a bunch of inventory – or making your own product. Believe it or not, you actually don't have to.

If you're willing to keep a *smaller* portion of your profits, you can upload your designs to a number of companies that will handle everything else. These are called Print on Demand platforms, and I'll briefly touch on a handful of them. There are a *lot* out there, but they aren't all going to be worth your time.

This is almost like drop shipping, and it's a very valid way to start printing and selling your t-shirts *right now*, with minimal startup costs. There are some downsides, though, so you need to keep profit margins, commissions, and fees in mind before you get it all started.

Spreadshop

Spreadshop is an offshoot of Spread*shirt*, and they have been doing online, on-demand merchandise for something like 15 years, which is truly eons in internet-time. The website is free to start using and very user-friendly.

With Spreadshop, you create an online storefront. You can customize it some to your brand, though not as much as if you were creating a full website. However, if you choose to have a website, *in addition*, Spreadshop has tools to help you integrate your site and its storefront.

You set your own price for your products, and their commission rates are some of the highest when it comes to companies like this. Unfortunately, that still means you're only getting about 20% from each sale. If your shop and designs take off, and you're selling in bulk, you can make as much as 40% from each product, though.

One of the benefits of Spreadshop is that they have numerous different items you can have your custom designs put onto, in addition to t-shirts. If you want bags, buttons, and mugs, too? You can do that, and it's not any extra.

Everything from the printing to the packing, along with the shipping, is handled through Spreadshop. If there is an issue with your product, they also take care of customer service.

This seems like a really great idea, and for many people who want to take a more passive approach, it can be! There are obvious downsides, though, including not be able to handle the product, having to work through the company, and obviously, only getting such a small portion of the sale amount.

CafePress

CafePress has also been around a while and works in a similar way to SpreadShop. You set up your storefront, upload your designs, and they handle printing, packing, and shipping.

At this moment, the base price for a CafePress shirt is $18. The rate changes as prices fluctuate. If you sell your products at $19, then you're making just $1 for each shirt. This is a fairly steep base price, especially considering that the quality isn't necessarily always there. Reviews vary, so this is simply anecdotal evidence.

Zazzle

Once again, Zazzle works in a way that is easy to use and set up – you upload your designs, and they handle printing, shipping, etc. Each shirt and design have a different 'predetermined' base price, and then you add your commission on top of that.

Zazzle recommends a 12% markup, but you can increase it anywhere from just 5% to 99%. Depending on your rate, a transaction fee is going to apply on top of that, eating into your profit again.

RedBubble

RedBubble doesn't have a set amount per shirt but instead will calculate how much the shirt will cost *them* based on quality and design. After that, you can set your mark up to determine how much you want to 'make' from each item you sell.

RedBubble is more of a "higher-end" choice, as they have a really excellent reputation for quality. This does mean you pay more for that, of course. Just like with our previous choices, RedBubble handles printing and shipping, so you never have to manage your own inventory.

Amazon Merch

I've saved what some consider the best for last, Amazon Merch. I don't think I need to tell you what an internet giant Amazon is – they get hundreds of millions of visitors each month literally, and it's a trusted shopping front. That means if you're selling your designs on Amazon, you already have a good leg up.

Just like with our previous sites, Amazon Merch lets you upload your designs, and they will handle the printing, shipping, and customer issues. You never have to handle your own products or inventory at all.

Just like with most of our suggested sites, it doesn't cost a thing to start an Amazon Merch account and start designing your shirts. You upload your designs to the site, pick a color – or a few colors – that work well. Then, you set up a title, a handful of bullet points in the description, and you can start selling it almost immediately.

Amazon does limit the number of shirt designs you're able to have, but as you sell and grow, they will open up more slots for you. Essentially, if you become a proven seller, they give you yet more opportunity to sell.

There are people online making an easy 5 figures a month just with their Amazon Merch account. I cannot stress enough how much being backed by the Amazon giant can help you propel your business.

Of course, there are always downsides – this isn't a foolproof method.

Amazon does not play when it comes to both copyright and trademark. If they catch you using a phrase that is trademarked, they will ban your entire account. If they catch you using a logo or design that is copyrighted, they will ban your entire account. You may not even mean to do these things, but it can happen.

You can search for your designs on the United States Patent and Trade Office, or USPTO, website, or on Trademarkia, a free online trademark search engine. While you absolutely should be doing this with every single design you make, if you accidentally slip up on Amazon, they will show you no mercy.

You might be wondering why *everyone* doesn't use Amazon Merch if they are so much better than other options. I saved this option for last because it's the newest option on the market. Compared to the lifespan of the others, the Merch option is the 'new kid' on the block. That's not to say that it isn't a good option – it's just *less* tested than some.

Amazon doesn't call the money you receive from each, say, a 'commission' like some companies do. Instead, they refer to it as *royalties*. Your royalties are based on each item you sell and range from $2.21 (for a shirt selling for $15.99) to $9.77 (for a shirt selling for $25.99) for a standard t-shirt design.

Shopify + Amazon Works

I'm going to *briefly* touch on this. Sometimes, the Amazon Merch app will go down, meaning that they stop accepting new sellers. This usually happens when they get a lot of applications, and you may have to wait several weeks *or* several months to get accepted into the program. Once you're accepted, it's a very fast process, but that initial wait is a bummer.

Instead, you *can* create a Shopify account and sell *through* Amazon using this account. This is a really great workaround, though it does take a few more steps.

You can set up a seller's account on Shopify for free using the free trial. You'll have to set up and pay for a full account at some point, but everything we're doing here works without paying anything upfront. This is a good way to start making money to help fund your business, too.

Once you have signed up for Shopify, head to the Apps section of the shop and find a well-reviewed shop that will do Print on Demand for you. This works pretty much like every other Print on Demand service we have talked about, where you are able to upload your designs, choose sizes and t-shirt information, and the company itself will handling all inventory, printing, and shipping.

I have used, and like, Teelaunch – but there are *numerous* apps that will work with this. When I did my research, Teelaunch offered the best product when you consider the return on investment and the quality you get. Feel free to do your own research with the apps to find something *you* like; this is only my own experience speaking here.

Once you've installed Teelaunch, go into the back end of your Shopify account. Hit the *Account* button on the top right, and fill out all the needed information – including a card. This card information is what will be charged each time you fill an order. Every 14 days, you will get your payment from Amazon for your sales, and you'll be able to pay off this card using that money – whatever is left over is your profit.

Alright, so you have Teelaunch (or your chosen application) installed, and you have the necessary card information set up. Now it's time to get your first design ready.

In the Teelaunch app, click on New Product, which should be at the very top of the page. Pick your preferred shirt (in my experience, the Gildan t-shirt is a great balance of quality and price), and upload your design.

The editor is very easy to use, and you will be able to adjust how and where it prints on the shirt. Choose the sizes you wish to offer and the colors you want your shirt or design in. Once you feel good about the final product, give it a title, a few description points, and hit publish.

It's really that easy – you've created a shirt in your

Shopify account. Once you feel good about it and you are ready for the next step, it's time to attach this to an Amazon account.

Back in Shopify, you're going to click on the *Add a Sales Channel* option on the left menu. Select Amazon, and install it in your account.

You do need an Amazon Sellers account in order to proceed. This is easy to set up on the site itself and costs $39.99/month at the time of writing. This is an upfront cost you can't get around. If you already have a Sellers account, you can use that.

Once everything is connected, go into the Amazon app and hit *Sell on Amazon.* You should be able to see the design you set up in Teelaunch that is currently on your Shopify account. Select that product, and fill out all the important information.

Because this isn't an Amazon Merch item, you're going to be creating your brand here. (I'll talk about the importance of branding soon, so stay tuned) You need to enter your brand information, the title of the shirt, a handful of bullet points that customers will see right away, plus a description. Use keywords that you know your customers would need to search for to find this shirt – if you're selling a t-shirt about vegan products or animal rights, use those words in the description!

Pro Tip: The bullet points on your page are pretty important! You're going to want to work keywords that revolve around your design within these bullet points without them sounding like a robot wrote it trying to stuff keywords into something. Be sure to read the sentences out loud to yourself to ensure they make sense. If someone is searching for your shirt, have you included words they might use to find your product?

Your bullet points should also *sell* your product. If your bullet points aren't compelling or interesting, there is a good chance that potential customers will click off your page before they even get to the actual description. As you're writing your bullet points, ask yourself: would I buy this product? Is this interesting? Compelling? Accurate? If the answer is no, rework it!

If this is your first shirt, you're going to need to do one

additional step, which is clicking the *Apply to Sell in This Category* box. It's going to ask a handful of questions, and then you'll immediately be approved. It's less of an application and more of a survey, honestly.

Minor Things You'll Need

When you sell this way on Amazon, you're going to need two things – a UPC and an SKU. The UPC is harder to come across, so I'll talk about that first.

UPC stands for Universal Product Code. These are standardized across the board, and Amazon requires them in order to be sold. They are unique codes to each product; you cannot reuse them. Honestly, you can get a handful of unused UPCs on eBay for less than $20, and it saves you a lot of hassle. You can also go through GS1US to get your own codes, though these do cost more upfront.

You also need an SKU. SKUs are for your internal information only, so you really can use a random 10-digit string of numbers. I record all my SKUs and UPCs in an Excel spreadsheet for my own records.

And... that's it! At this point, you should be able to hit publish. Within an hour, your item will be up for sale on Amazon's website.

What About Shipping?

I almost forgot! You need to ensure your seller settings are right and up to date, so you are charging the appropriate amount of shipping – and letting your customers know how long it will take.

In your Seller Central Account, be sure you are charging enough to cover Teelaunch's shipping and handling fees. Think about the price that your customer will want to pay while you still make a profit. I always extend Teelaunch's shipping estimate by a few days (if Teelaunch tells me it takes 7 days to ship a shirt, I tell my customers 10, just so there is plenty of wiggle room). I also tend to lower shipping, which means I am eating a bit of the shipping costs myself, but I find more people are willing to purchase with a lower shipping cost.

If my shirt is selling for $17 on Amazon with $3 shipping, the customer is paying $20, right? Through Teelaunch, with my preferred shirt and design, they are charging me about $12 for a printed and shipped shirt.

Amazon has a fee on top of that, which is just over $3. We can round down and say that each shirt sold through Amazon is making me $4.

That might seem low to you, and I understand your knee-jerk reaction of being disappointed. However, now that the design is made and uploaded, it's completely automated. I can work on and upload another design and make another $4 per shirt.

Amazon is the biggest shopping market in the world, and you could potentially reach millions of eyes each day. If 5 people buy at least one shirt from my store each day, that is $20/day or $140/week. I'm *not* doing any active work on this. Once it is set up, you can literally walk away and forget about it. As long as you remember to pay the Amazon fees, it just sits and makes a passive profit.

The more designs you have and the better niches you get into, the more money you can make. It's not hard to make 5 figures a month *completely passively* with this system, especially once you get it down. The longer you're at it, the more money you're able to make.

How to Create Your Designs

You may already be a graphic designer, and this section doesn't apply to you. If you're *not,* and you're not entirely sure how to start making your designs into a reality, I can offer you some advice that has worked for me. Because no, I'm *also* not a graphic designer by trade, but that hasn't stopped me yet.

Your first option is to learn to do it yourself! YouTube is an amazing resource, and most programs – even the free ones – have some basic tutorials built into them that you can use to learn the ropes. After that, it's a lot of experimentation to find what you like and how to craft your designs.

GIMP is the best free program on the market for this, in my opinion. It's very powerful, it's relatively easy to use, and you can produce high-quality images without a lot of hassle.

If you already have a Photoshop or Illustrator account, this is a great option – but these will cost upfront if you don't have an account, so keep that in mind! For many smaller operations, it's really not worth the big financial investment to get a Photoshop account.

Canva is also a free online program that will help you create satisfying designs, and it's even easier to pick up than GIMP. However, there are limitations on what Canva can create, including limitations on the size of the design.

Speaking of size, if you are *uploading* your design to be printed, like on CafePress or Amazon Merch, remember that bigger is better. When it is smaller and 'squished,' you're going to be able to still get those crisp lines and edges.

Shoot for something like 4500x5400 to get that perfect image. Customers will notice if your design has fuzzy edges or an imperfect edge.

You Can Also Outsource

While I absolutely recommend you to start creating on your own *first*, you can also outsource your design. The internet is a wonderful thing, and it's full of Photoshop pros and graphic designers who would love to exchange money for designs.

The more design ideas you're able to give a designer at one time, the better the final result will be. If you have a niche or a design in mind, do everything you can to convey your needs to the designer.

Go in with specifics, but know that they will also have their own artistic license to make it unique – *especially* if you're sending them examples and asking them for 'their own take' on a design.

Sites like Guru, UpWork, and Fiverr are going to be your best starter places for finding a good designer. You're not going to be the first person to think about outsourcing this work – many, many t-shirt designers outsource the graphic design work to a professional. It can cost anywhere from $4-$10 for a design, depending on how many you want and how much work that design is.

Do not ask for something vague, like "shirts about pets." Be specific in what you want and what you are going to do with the final image. If you don't necessarily have the perfect idea *in mind*, offer them links and samples to pull inspiration from. As long as the final product is unique, not a copy, this is a great way to get a unique design within your niche.

What is a Target Audience, and Do I Need One?

I'm going to talk a lot about target audiences in this book, so this is a pretty important section in the book. I would also probably argue that *every* section is an important section, but nailing down your target market and knowing *who* you are going to be selling to is very important. This is going to influence many other steps you take in the business, including your final product, your marketing, and more.

I want you to pause for a moment and think about who you want to sell your t-shirts to. Are you thinking about funny, punny shirts for the average gym-goer? Are you thinking about a soft, durable t-shirt as a lifestyle brand? Are you going to want to do video game t-shirts, so you need a durable shirt that will take more intricate designs?

Your target market is just that – the part of the market you want to target. Think about your ideal customer and who they are.

Your first knee-jerk reaction is probably going to be that *everyone* is your target market. You want to sell to everyone! That's fine in theory. However, in *practice*, when you try to appeal to everyone, you end up appealing to no one. Becoming too broad, especially at first, is just going to hurt you in the long run. It's better to target 5,000 people who are perfect for your product than 500,000 people who are probably not interested.

When you're thinking about this question (and I hope you give it a good, long thought!), I want you to answer these questions.

What is the age range of my ideal buyer?

What does my ideal buyer do for a living?

What level of education do you think your ideal buyer has?

Are they married? Single? Engaged? Do they have children?

Where do they live? Inside the US, out of the US? Where are they from?

This might sound like *a lot* of things to take into mind, but the more you can nail down your target market, the easier time you will have at selling your product! As you're answering these questions, you can think about your product line and your products.

By the end of answering all of these questions, you probably have a better idea of the types of things you're going to be selling and who is going to buy them.

Your product is absolutely going to drive your market. If you want to sell athletic shirts to 20 and 30-something gymgoers who like hiking on the weekend, you will probably want to focus on shirts with an athletic material that breathes well. If your target market, though, works in an office and spends their weekends shopping at thrift stores and enjoying cheesy TV shows, athletic tank tops are not going to sell well.

Pro tip: For folks that are struggling with their target market, I encourage you to think about focusing on yourself. Who are you, and what would you buy? Are you selling shirts you would want to purchase? This might be a good starting point for you!

What's Your Niche?

While you're thinking about your target market, your niche is going to come into play. Finding a good niche is very important, and just like your target market, it's going to drive many aspects of your business plan, your marketing plan, and more.

A niche is essentially just a specialized, narrow segment of the marketplace. Someone who only makes the ampersand shirts? That's a niche. Someone, that only sells funny pet shirts? That's a niche, too! Finding your own niche is going to help you work on your target market more, perfect your product, and ultimately sell the best product possible.

Underserved Niches are Best

This is a little bit common sense, but a lot of people get so caught up in an idea or concept that they forget about this. If your ideal niche is oversaturated and too many people are selling similar products, you're going to have a hard time gaining traction, *especially* as you first start out.

Ideally, your niche will be heavily *under*served. Your target market should have a need or desire for your product, and no one will be selling something quite like what you have. However, some people *do* find success with markets that have relatively high saturation points. They could find success with a higher quality product, a better price point, or some combination of those.

Ultimately, the more you can stand out from the crowd and set yourself apart in your niche and with your target market, the better you are going to be.

Using Amazon to Find Your Niches

Let's say you know you want to create novelty pet shirts. That's fun! Everyone loves dogs, after all, and your target market owns and loves pets.

If you're struggling with figuring out what might sell, what works, and what is already out there, do an Amazon search for "pet novelty shirt" and use the left options to filter out the actual clothes for pets, leaving men's novelty shirts.

With this, you're able to see the products that *Amazon* is selling. When you click on each individual product, scroll down until you see a box with a sales ranking.

What you should be paying attention to here is the Amazon Best Sellers Rank, or BSR. The BSR indicates how many of these items are sold. With this information, you can determine how popular a design like this is.

In general, the lower the BSR, the more shirts the

company is selling each day. A BSR of between 100,0
and 300,000 means the shirt is selling between 1 an
times each day. The lower the number, the more these
shirts are selling.

This is going to give you a really good idea of the market
for this *type* of shirt. If there are many similar shirts that
are all selling well, perhaps this market is a little oversaturated.

I recommend you looking at *several* niches and even
several brands to see what they sell and how they have
branched out. This should help you get a 'base' idea of
what people love and where you can your products can fit
into the market.

You can also do similar searching on platforms like Etsy
or CafePress. These searches are important to help
determine who your competition might be and what they
are selling. You really shouldn't go into this blind without
knowing what others are selling.

Note: I have found that the best niches are niches that
people themselves are passionate about.

Environmentalism, kids, pets... if someone feels very strongly about a topic, they are more likely to advertise that on their body.

If you're really struggling, I encourage you to browse Google Trends to see what people are searching for in their daily life. The "bestseller" or "most popular" sections of RedBubble and Zazzle are also great resources and will help you get a feel for what *other* people are selling. You know there is a market if they are selling them, after all!

Another great way to do more research into your niche is to look if there is a subreddit for your niche. Simply searching "dog Reddit," "vegan Reddit," or "your desired topic + Reddit" should be enough to find what you're looking for.

See what users are interested in. Find out what they like, what designs or topics or funny sayings they use regularly.

What can you easily translate to a shirt in order to sell to these folks?

Are they within your target market? Is it a very small community – a few hundred to a few thousand – or is it a very large and active community?

This will help determine how viable your niche is and the potential interest in your product.

What is a Brand? Do I Need One?

If you're going to be creating t-shirts using a process like Amazon Merch, CafePress, or RedBubble, your branding is going to be slightly less important. However, if you are planning on creating your own shop, using Shopify with Amazon, or presenting *yourself*, branding is absolutely essential.

A big part of your marketing and online presence is going to revolve around your brand. You should start thinking about your brand *right now* before you even design a shirt or start an online account. Your brand is your identity, your persona, and the backbone of your business. Every decision you make when it comes to website design to t-shirt design, logo design, and more is going to be influenced by your branding.

Before you settle on any of your brandings, you need to make sure you're taking into consideration your target market and what they will find appealing. I warned you, we're going to talk about target markets a lot.

If your target market finds your brand or your identity boring or undesirable, they won't want to buy your products, let alone wear them. On the flip side, if your target market identifies with your brand, they are going to *want* to wear your shirts and represent you in public. This is obviously the ideal outcome.

When you're thinking about branding, you want to make sure you distance yourself from anything negative. This sounds obvious, but it's *really easy* to get caught up in wanting to be cute, funny, or push the envelope to help set yourself apart from the crowd. If this appeals to your target market, you may be able to get away with it a bit, but you don't want to go do so much that you will turn off everyone.

Wait, what does my logo have to do with negativity?

Branding is so much more than a name and a logo or a website design. Your branding is the message you're sending to your consumers, flat out. It's important that you are able to convey your message loud and clear and with positivity.

Take out that notebook I told you to keep close a few chapters ago, and start thinking about answers to these questions. You don't have to answer them all, but brainstorming about your brand and your mission is going to make it a lot easier to get your brand and your store off the ground. The clearer your brand is, the more users will identify with you and your message and the more interested they will be in buying your products.

Who are you, as a brand? As a company? As an owner? You're not another faceless corporation with millions of dollars in funding; you're just a person with a dream and a goal. Make sure your customers know that.

What do you do, and why? You make t-shirts, obviously. But why? The majority of brand stories have the owner (you) facing an issue, and they have *fixed* that issue for the consumer. It could be you wanted funny, attractive gym clothes at affordable prices.

It could be that you're very passionate about a certain cause, and you want to share that with the world. Whatever it is, present it like it is an issue, and only you can fix it.

Who are you doing this for? Who is your target market? Is it people that also love pets or feel passionately about your cause? Are you trying to support someone?

What is your process? How have you created your products? This is probably the most fun part to write. Share with your consumer how you have created your products. If you're using a company to produce the shirts and not handling inventory, you can talk instead about how you have created your designs, the inspiration behind them, or why they are meaningful to you.

Really, this is just another way to humanize yourself and your brand and let the customer know they're supporting a small business.

Once you're written down your rough answers, I encourage you to go back and format them in an easy-to-read way. This can translate in the *About Us* section of your website and will let your customers know who you are and what you stand for. It doesn't have to be a novella of your life story! Short, sweet, and to the point should be the goal.

Whether you're thinking about a website design or a logo, a description, or a name for a t-shirt, you should always keep your *brand* and your *target market* in mind.

Would your target market like/appreciate this? Does this feel on-brand? If the honest answer is no, you need to go back to the drawing board.

Take a look at companies like Dannijo, AirBnB, Burt's Bees, Everlane, and even Nike to see what I mean about branding and having a voice. Read their stories, learn about the company, and see if you can notice how their values and their concept translate into things like marketing, logos, design, and more.

A clear branding message is absolutely the way to go.

Selling Online: The Ins, The Outs, The Important Things

Thinking about selling your products online? If you're handling your own inventory, there's a good chance you're going to want to hit more of your target market... unless your target market is an old folk home, the internet is probably the best way to do that. (Note: my own mother is in an old folk's home, and she still knows how to navigate a site and put her credit card information in!)

There are a few different options for selling online, but we'll talk about all of them briefly and how you can make the most out of whatever platform you choose.

How To Really Sell Your Product – Mock-ups

I don't know about you, but I'm significantly more likely to purchase something like an item of clothing if I can see a person wearing it. I know I'm not alone, either – it's a lot easier to visualize what an item of clothing looks like when you can actually see it *on another person.*

This is really hard to do, however, when you're starting an online business. Hiring models and photographers isn't cheap, and depending on how many products you have in your store, it can get out of hand quickly. Photos taken on most phones, even higher-end ones, don't necessarily look professional, though and 'good enough' probably isn't what you're going for.

These options aren't your only choices, believe it or not.

You're not the first person to run into this issue, and there are online tools out there just for you and your brand new t-shirt business. There are actually websites out there that allow you to use *their* models and *their* images to showcase your designs.

They are called t-shirt mock-ups and templates, and there are a number of websites that let you do this.

If you have your files in Photoshop, which is the most common, you can use the sites GraphicRiver or MockupWorld. If you are using one of the other options, so your files are in a different format, Printful and Printify are both really excellent options for you.

Most of these are *very* easy to use. You simply choose the t-shirt that is most like yours, upload your image, and center it on the model as it would print on an actual t-shirt. The site helps blend your design into the folds and wrinkles of the shirt the model is wearing, and the final product really *does* look like the model you've chosen is wearing your shirt.

Depending on the site you ultimately choose, there are a

variety of body types, shirt types, and models to choose from. This is a really great way to lend credibility to your product and help it stand out *without* spending the money on an actual model and photographer.

I have *personally* used both Printful and GraphicRiver. My preference is GraphicRiver, both for the price and the quality of images, but you should choose what looks best with *your* design and fits into *your* budget! Use what works for *you* and what you like to use.

Etsy

Etsy is probably the biggest crafting platform online right now, and if you're making your own shirts, you're probably considering selling through Etsy. That makes sense – Etsy gets literally *hundreds of millions* of site views each month according to SimilarWeb, and ranks around 32 in the most popular websites to get traffic within the United States.

It just *makes sense* to have a presence on Etsy, but starting a storefront there can be a little intimidating. The good news, it's not *actually* hard to get yourself set up and start selling nearly immediately.

Before you jump into Etsy, be sure you understand the fees that you're going to be paying. Of course, there are fees for using their platform – few things in life are free.

Each time you list an item for sale, no matter if it *sells* or not, you're going to be spending a few. Every 4 months, you need to 'renew' that listing, so it stays live, and you pay that fee again.

There is also a base transaction fee for each sale on Etsy. At the time of writing, that fee is 5%, but it has changed in the past, so be sure to check before signing up. This means for every $100 in t-shirts you sell, you'll be giving Etsy $5. That's a fairly low fee, all things considered, but depending on your volume, it can really add up fast.

Your Etsy store should fit in with your branding, and it should absolutely fit your target market. You know – theoretically – what your target market likes. Be sure to take advantage of all the branding opportunities Etsy has, which are a lot. You can have a custom store logo, store banner, and even a cover photo. The owner photo isn't strictly necessary, but when shopping on Etsy, most people like knowing they are supporting small artisans. A good owner photo helps with that.

Selling on Facebook Marketplace

This is a fairly common way for new business owners and crafters to try and get their feet wet. The benefits of using Facebook Marketplace are that it's free to post, and you are selling to people in your own community. If that is your target market – those local to you – this is a really great idea.

There are a few things to keep in mind, and the first thing is safety. You're meeting strangers from the internet, and that can be shady. You can offer to ship, but some people are unwilling to pay – if you do local pickup, always choose a public location during the day. I know, I sound like your mother – but you truly never know who you are selling to or who you are meeting. Just be safe.

Facebook groups are also a good option. They work a little different from the marketplace, but if your target market is local to you, or you want to reach local buyers, a community group is also a great place to start.

Be sure that you pay attention to the rules of the group, as self-promotion is usually limited. Don't try to skirt the rules and end up kicked out of the group!

Another Option: Selling at Local Events

Farmers markets? Flea markets? Local pop-up events featuring local artisans? This is an amazing resource for you if you want to sell locally!

Setting up your table and getting your supplies the *first* time is going to be the biggest upfront expense, but once you have everything you need, you shouldn't have too many rolling expenses. Just the cost of getting a table and the time it takes you to sit there, smile politely, and sell your goods.

The biggest tip I can give you if you're selling in person is to make your table look *good*! If your goods are hard to see, disorganized, or not even on display, how are people supposed to know what you're selling or if you have good quality products? This is partially about branding yourself properly, but also about just common sense. If your table looks good, people will want to buy from you.

Another important thing some people don't consider is their personal temperament. Are you a people person? Do you naturally smile when someone walks up to you? Do you have the ability to answer the same 3-5 questions *over and over* again?

If you don't, selling in person at a market or event may not be for you. That sounds harsh? Perhaps! But you need to be honest with yourself. Some people really just don't have the temperament to do this, and that is okay. You don't want to scare your customers off with a blunt comment or a frustrating afternoon. You *will* be asked the same questions over and over again, and it can get really frustrating, especially when it's 90 degrees out and you're ready to just be home.

That said, if you're a people person and selling at markets or fairs sounds appealing to you, there are a lot of advantages. It's a great stepping point between selling online and selling in a physical store, and you have a lot of great networking opportunities built into something like this. Who knows who you are going to meet, honestly, and what their needs are. It's totally possible that you could find a local company or organization in need of your skills, and you may end up making shirts for a local organization.

Don't discount the connections you make! You never know what is going to come out of it.

Creating Your Own Website

If you're going to be making your own shirts and handling your own inventory, you're probably going to need a way to sell online. A website is going to be the most personalized way to do that.

A lot of people feel very overwhelmed when they think about starting their own website, probably because it used to be very hard! The good news is you need to know pretty much zero HTML (or HyperText Markup Language) to get your website off the ground… and it doesn't have to cost hundreds of dollars and cause a lot of headaches.

There are plenty of free online platforms you can use to set up your website, and it doesn't have to be intimidating. WordPress is the biggest platform on the web, and it's also very easy to use.

There are a lot of options online for a "free" website hosting service, but you shouldn't go with "good enough," especially if you're selling your product. When it comes to getting your domain name and your hosting service, be sure you pay for your own domain. Nothing turns me off more from giving a site my credit card than sitename.weeboo.com!

Bluehost is often recommended. I've had great results with them, as well as NameCheap.

Next, be sure you utilize WordPress plugins *and* themes. There are a variety of themes and plugins available, both free and paid, for online storefronts. Find a theme that fits the brand that you identify with – the final product is so important!

If you feel very uncomfortable doing this process yourself, you can absolutely hire your website creation out to a professional. Check on websites like Fiverr and UpWork to find a reputable developer with good reviews. Be sure you talk with them before you hire them, so they really understand your vision and your brand.

The clearer you are with your needs at the start of the project, the better your final product is going to be. It sounds obvious when I say it, but so many people contact freelance web developers asking for something vague or unhelpful and hoping for magic. The more direction someone has, the better your website will be!

Prices for this can range from a hundred dollars to a few thousand depending on how much you need to be done and who you choose for the job. I encourage you to find someone that you're comfortable with that also fits within your budget.

How to Sell on Your Website

If you have a website, I'm going to guess the main motive is to sell your t-shirts. It's not nearly as hard to start an online store for your site as you think it is.

The most popular option right now on the web is, without a doubt, Shopify. Shopify has gained a huge following over the last several years, and it has become the go-to way for smaller shops to set up a storefront quickly and easily.

Shopify legitimately makes it *incredibly easy* to set up a storefront, and if you get lost, the Shopify Blog is actually very helpful. You can make it, so you simply copy and paste information from Shopify to your website, and your store will function, or you can set up a shop within Shopify and use their web service. The volume you're doing and the amount of time you want to spend will dictate what works for you, but I like using my own website for customization and simply utilizing Shopify's buying tools to handle payment processing.

Shopify also helps you manage inventory, so you don't accidentally oversell, and it has a lot of tools for new businesses. If you're worried about this, be sure to check out what they can offer you!

Before you take your site live and go with the next steps, I want you to walk through everything and really think – is this easy to navigate? Does this site make sense? If you are a customer seeing it for the first time, can you find what you're looking for? Does it make you want to purchase?

What About Taking Payment?

There are a lot of other ways to take payment, however. If you're not interested in Shopify – I'm not affiliated with them in any way; I just know about their products and know many people who use them! - there are other options out there for you.

PayPal is one of the oldest ways to do business, and a lot of folks still use their tools for a reason. PayPal is incredibly secure, and it protects not just you as the seller but also the buyer.

When someone buys through PayPal, they know the company has their back if something goes wrong – which ultimately makes the customer feel a lot more secure about their purchase.

PayPal will let you add a *buy now* button from your business account that will record the sale and take the payment for you. It's very easy, even if you're not a very technical person.

Stripe is another popular option, and they allow local currencies as well as Bitcoin, which is pretty cool if your target market is into that. They also have reoccurring billing, which might appeal to some businesses, and fraud protection.

Pay with Amazon is a relatively new option for some businesses and offers the same protections as Stripe. Square is also fairly popular online, and in addition to all the benefits like fraud protection and easy placement on your website, Square has options to let you take payment *in person*, too, with a card.

If you are selling in person and want to be able to take a credit card, there is a good chance that Square is going to be the best option for you when you first start out.

It's important to remember that **no matter what** system you use to take payment, there will be *some* fees associated with it.

Every company has to take its own cut, and you're probably not going to be getting 100% of your sale price unless you're selling in person for cash only. This limits your market a *lot*, obviously. When you are pricing your shirts, always keep in mind sales fees. These eat into your bottom line but are a necessary evil!

What is a Business Plan, and Do I Need One?

I get it – you're not a multimillion-dollar company with a full board of members, investors, and more. You're... well, you, probably, with maybe a good friend or family member there to help you out when you need an extra hand.

However, you still need a business plan.

I encourage you to *not* zone out for this chapter and skim it. I understand this isn't all that exciting, especially after I probably fried your brain with tax information, but it's incredibly important. You want to set yourself up for success, right? Well, this is a big part of it!

A business plan is so important because it indicates you have direction, drive, and you know what you're doing... think of a good business plan as a road map to success. You wouldn't go on a road trip without a map, a guide, or directions, right? At least, not if you have a specific destination in mind. Building your business is the same, so be sure you're starting off right.

I'm going to ask you questions about *your specific* business, about where you want to go, and how you want to get there. Write down these questions and any answers you have. Really think about it, and take some time when answering. You don't have to have all the answers right away, but eventually, you will need to answer them all.

The Backbone of a Good Business Plan

Personally, I believe the core of a good business plan comes from *goals*. What are your short-term goals for the business? Long-term goals? Where do you see the business in 5 years? 10 years?

If you don't have answers for this yet, that is totally okay. This is what I'm here to help with.

I'm going to start by saying there is *no* wrong answer here. If you decide you want this to just be a side hustle to make some passive income and help you pay off some debt or build a future, *that's okay*. If you want to quit your job and make this a full-time gig where you can grow, that's okay too! Just be honest.

Dreaming big is great, but we're going to work on not necessarily tamping down the dream but making it more realistic and more attainable. Not everyone is going to create a t-shirt empire and retire at 32, and that's totally okay! I'm about to teach you how to create realistic, positive goals that will help push you to success.

Using the SMART Goals System

This is something that is taught in business courses to help potential business owners or managers create realistic goals and then hit them.

You don't need a business degree, however, to use SMART goals to your advantage. I'll break down how to set and achieve your business goals using SMART.

I'm not yelling the word *smart* at you, I swear. SMART is an acronym, and it stands for **specific, measurable, achievable, relevant, and time-bound**. These are the criteria that I want you to use when you're thinking and creating business goals.

Each and every goal should be SMART, in that is a specific goal that is measurable in its progress and success, achievable by you and your business, relevant to you and your business, and time-bound in that you know when it needs to be completed.

If you're still a little lost or need some guidance, I can assist more.

What a Specific Goal Means

When creating your goals, they need to specific. Avoid any vague misunderstandings or loose guidelines.

I want to be a millionaire.

I want to make enough money from this business to send my kids to school.

I want to quit my day job.

All great goals, sure, but none are very specific. You need to nail down the exact specifications for your best results. **What** do you want to accomplish, *exactly*? **What** is your ideal outcome from this goal? **Where** can you make this goal a reality? **Why** is this goal important to you? **Why** is this goal important to the business? **What** is going to be involved, exactly, in accomplishing this goal? **Who** is going to be involved in this?

For every single goal you set for yourself and your business, I want you to dig into these questions. This might mean that your goal moves from a few words to a few sentences, but that is okay! The more specific you get, the more likely you are to be able to accomplish it.

What a Measurable Goal Means

If you can't measure your goals, is there really a point to having goals at all? That might sound a little dramatic, but it's totally true. As important as specific goals are *measurable* goals, where you can say for sure that you are making progress and when you have succeeded and hit your goals.

With each goal you're creating, ask yourself how many? How much? How far? Will I know when I hit the halfway point? Will I know when I hit the goal?

If the answers are no, then your goals are not measurable. Or at least, they aren't measurable *enough*.

The danger of not creating a measurable goal is that you never truly hit it. This can be incredibly discouraging – which I'll talk about in a minute when I yet again tell you how important SMART is.

What an Achievable Goal Means

Sit down and be honest with yourself for a minute. Can you actually achieve this goal? I'm not trying to be a jerk to you – I'm trying to give you a dose of reality.

When you make goals like "I want to make 14 million in my 3rd year", well, your dreams are there, but it's *probably not going to happen*. Again, I'm not being a jerk – I'm bringing you back into reality.

When you're making goals for your business, you need to make sure that you can actually achieve them. Otherwise, you are already setting yourself up for failure. Why would you ever want to do that?! Don't set yourself up for failure, or you're never going to beat the statistics and last.

What a Relevant Goal Means

This is probably the vaguest portion of the SMART goals, but it's just as important as the others. If your goals are not relevant to your business, your market, and, honestly, your personal life, you're never going to achieve them. Yet again, setting yourself up for failure.

Is your goal relevant to your business right now? Will your goal be relevant to your business in 5 years? Is your goal relevant to your target market? What about your products, and what you sell?

What a Time-Bound Goal Means

Finally, we've hit the end – the time-bound goals. This seems obvious to some folks, but not to us all – and it's easy to ignore this one.

When you're creating a goal, you need to ask yourself *when* it's going to be completed. One week? One month? One year?

Something like "sell x number of t-shirts" *seems* like a fine goal, but if you have no end date, there is no urgency. "Sell x shirts by y date" is a much better goal because it is *time-bound*.

Every day, every time you're thinking about your goals, ask yourself – when can this be done? What can I do today to help accomplish these goals? What do I need to do this week/month/year to achieve my goal?

Every Goal, Use This System

Goals are a backbone of a good business plan, so every time you create a goal for yourself or your business, refer back to the SMART system. For each goal you make, ask yourself – is this specific enough? Is this time-bound? Is this relevant?

I know this sounds like a lot to think about, but if you're not setting good goals for your business, *you are not* going to hit them. If you're not hitting your goals, it's very easy to get very discouraged quickly. If you're getting discouraged, you're probably not going to keep pushing towards your goals... and we all know where that leads.

What Else Do You Need With a Business Plan?

A business plan isn't just a goal, but that is very important. A business plan is, as the name suggests, a plan that helps guide you through the steps of growing your business. A good business plan should basically give the reader everything they need to know about your business. If I come into your business plan blind, I should be able to read it and know everything I need to by the end.

It's important to know there is no right or wrong way to write a business plan, and the way you write it should feel natural. While traditional business plans are very structured, they can be *dozens and dozens* of pages long and may feel too overwhelming for your small startup.

Elements of a Traditional Business Plan

A very traditional business plan starts with an *executive summary*, which is just a brief overview of what your company is and why it's going to be successful. Your mission statement, products you will offer, and any other basic information – like who *you* are and who else you'll be working with – should be included.

Wait, What's a Mission Statement? Do I Need One?

Alright, alright, let's back up *again* a moment. No matter how you write your business plan, you probably need a mission statement. A mission statement is basically a statement – a sentence to a few paragraphs – that describes the business's purpose. What you do and why you do it is your mission statement.

This doesn't have to be long; you don't have to get into all of the details. That isn't what this is for. This is simply to provide a solid framework for your business and your goals, essentially.

When you're writing a mission statement, answer the questions *why you exist* and *what makes you different*. Find a balance between realistic outlooks and optimism in your final goals.

Examples of Excellent, Short, To-The-Point Mission Statements

Warby Parker's mission statement is: To offer designer eyewear at a revolutionary price while leading the way for socially conscious businesses.

What a mission statement, right?! It's clear immediately what they are doing and what their end goal is, and I love it.

Honest Tea's mission statement is: To create and promote great-tasting, healthy, organic beverages.

Easy, to the point, and encompasses the major points of their business – to create something delicious that is good *for* you, too.

Ikea's mission statement is: To create a better everyday life for many people.

Ikea achieves its mission statement every single day by providing affordable, useful products for all sorts of people.

Telsa's mission statement is: To accelerate the world's transition to sustainable energy.

No matter how you feel about Tesla, you can't deny they are working hard to achieve their mission statement each and every day.

Back to your Business Plan... a Company Description

After your executive summary, a company description usually comes. This gives the reader detailed information about your company, more than the shorter introduction of the summary. This is also where you can show off a little bit. What makes you qualified to run this company? Are you passionate? Do you have a good background, artistic or business or otherwise?

Market Analysis

If you're just starting out, this might not be the easiest section to write, but it's pretty important. This is where you put the breakdown of your target market and your perfect customer. We have talked about this before, it shouldn't be a surprise!

If you have done market research into your competitors and your industry. What trends are you seeing that you want to capitalize on? What are others doing that is successful that you plan to adopt? What can do you *better* than they can? Break it down.

Organization, Management, and Business Structure

There is a good chance when you're first starting out; this isn't going to be long. Why? Because it's just you!

However, you're going to want to break down the structure of the business, who will be running it, and who will be responsible for what. If you have several people helping you out or working with you, laying out an organizational chart of who is in charge of whom and when can be helpful.

This is also the section where you should be detailing the *type* of business you have, which should be an LLC but might be a sole-proprietorship, depending on what route you went.

Your Product Line

Briefly touch on the types of products you're going to offer and the product lines you plan out, not just to have immediately but what you see yourself doing in the future. What are your product line goals?

Marketing Plans

This one is a little harder for new business owners to get, but you should briefly outline your marketing plans and desires. How are you going to find customers? How will you connect with them? How will you keep customers you already have and get repurchases?

You don't have to lay out a 25-point step on how to make your customers happy, but let everyone reading your business plan know you have *some type* of marketing plan and ideas in place.

Finance Requests? Put Them Here

I'm going to talk about investors and funding in a second, so hang tight, but if you're crafting your business plan to ask for funding, put that in here. This is where you talk about how much funding you need, ideally, over the next 3-7 years, and more importantly, what you are going to use your funding for.

Do you want debt? Do you want to offer equity instead? Are you buying materials? Equipment? Investing in training? Getting a building? Renting or owning? Paying salaries?

You need to be *very, very* specific if you fill out this section. People aren't just going to hand you money without a plan.

Financial Projections

This is going to get a bit complicated but stick with me here. When you first start your business, figuring out financial projections can be hard, but they are basically your projected sales and expected income.

If you are writing this section out once your business is already formed, you should be including balance sheets and cash flow statements. If you sold x amount in quarter one and y amount in quarter two, we could estimate that with similar growth, you will sell z in quarter three. Does that make sense?

Use any graphs you can put together and tell a visual story about your income and your growth. This is great for those just looking at your documents at a glance.

If you *don't* have any projections because you haven't sold a product yet, keep this short and simple. How much do you have to sell to turn a profit each day? What profit are you making from each item you sell?

Appendix

If you want, you can close your traditional business plan with an appendix, which is really just there to provide any additional supporting documents. Sometimes if you are requesting funding, investors will ask for more specifics. This is how you give it to them. Some include credit histories, your personal resumes, permits, any legal documents, any contracts you have, that sort of thing.

The Other Side of Business Plans: Short and Sweet

If the very traditional business plan doesn't appeal to you, well, I get it. It's long, and it's kind of boring, and it's a lot. If you are seeking funding from traditional sources or you plan to soon, I encourage you to take the time and effort to put together something like that.

However, if you are not requesting funding and no one but you and perhaps your partners or employees will see your business plan, you have other options. I'll never tell you to skip putting together a business plan altogether because I do believe it is important; you can a leaner, mean, start-up style plan that cuts all the fat from the business plan, leaving the most important 'bones.'

There are a lot of different ways to write one of those. I'll go over some of the most important things, but you should be adding what *you* think is important when it comes to running your business.

What **partnerships** you have, including those helping you run your business as well as any manufacturers you are going to be working closely with.

Activities you are going to be doing. What is giving you an edge over your competitors? What are you doing right that you think they are doing wrong? How can you be better?

Resources you are going to offer your customers or that you will be using to better yourself and your business.

The **value** you bring as a company and what you have to offer. This is where I would put your mission statement, and yes, you should still have a mission statement.

How will you be **interacting with customers**? What sort of relationships are you building? Is this in person? All online? How will you retain the customers you have and make them feel valued?

What experience are you providing your customers? I get it; you're selling t-shirts, not reinventing the wheel, but these are the things that separate businesses that are *fine* from those that are killing it.

In this section, you should also touch on the **channels** you'll be reaching your customers. Is this social media? Will you be sending out emails, too?

Who is your **target market** and **ideal customer**? Who do you want to sell to, and why?

Your **cost structure** is also important. How do you balance quality versus quantity? Are you looking to cut as many corners as you can or maximize the value that you are offering your customers? Is there a balance there?

Finally, you should always include your **revenue** plan. How much are you making from your product lines? What is your bottom line to keep the lights on, so to speak? What products are you offering?

Bottom Line on Business Plans

They're boring to write, they're probably boring to read, and it's not really exciting. It's not the fun and glamorous part of owning a business that you dreamed of; *I get that.* However, it's so important.

It's so important! You need to be sure you are absolutely nailing this and writing out a detailed and comprehensive business plan.

Just like when you're creating the right goals, having the right road map is going to give you the best chance at success. When you don't know where you are and where you're going, you are so much less likely to find proper success.

Writing out a business plan also helps keep everything in perspective, helps you understand what you *don't* know yet about your new business and what you need to do. If *nothing else*, writing out a business plan gets you in the right headspace to then *run that business.*

The Nitty Gritty: Bank Accounts, LLC, Taxes, and More Boring Things You Need to Know About

This really isn't anyone's idea of fun, but we're going to take a pause and talk about making it all legal and above board. If you're moving forward with your business and you're ready to get started making money, you need to get all of this sorted out.

Don't panic! It's not all that complicated. Okay, it's a little complicated, and it's very important. But it's very important to get right, so I'm going to walk you through step by step to ensure that you don't miss something, and come tax time, you are setting yourself up for success. No one wants a fight with the IRS, after all.

Choosing a Business Name

First thing is first, let's think about your business name. There is a lot that goes into your name, but you probably already have an idea of a company name in mind. Honestly, that's one of the first things people think about when they're dreaming of starting on their own.

As always, think about both your target market and your branding when coming up with a name. Does it suit you? Does it suit your brand? Will your customers like it, identify with it, appreciate it? Does it *make sense* for what type of shirts and products you're selling?

Once you've got an idea – or several ideas – for a name, you should check out your state's business records. These should be available online and fairly easy to search through, depending on your state. Make sure that no one has already registered your ideal name with your state for their own business. If they have, well, it's back to the drawing board.

If you're clear in your state, head to your county *and* the state trademark records. If your name is trademarked by someone else, you obviously can't use it for your own business. You should also check if someone has a name that is *very close* to yours doing something similar. Obviously, that isn't ideal.

Once you've got a name that no one else has, it's time to register it!

You need to file a *DBA* or a Doing Business As registration. This is basically stating your intent to do business under this name. Check with your local county website to fill this out, and be sure you're doing it with the county you're working in.

Once you've registered your DBA, it's time to think about how you want to own your company. You do want to own it, right?

Why an LLC is For You

There are two ways to handle your business: you can have something called a sole-proprietorship, or you can have an LLC. The subhead probably lets you know what I suggest, but I'll touch on both for a minute.

A sole-proprietorship is basically saying yes, this is my business, I own it, I take responsibility, I do it all. On the surface, this sounds like the right choice, right? I mean, you *are* the owner. You *are* the one responsible. With a sole-proprietorship, you don't even have to file taxes separately as a business; it all just rolls right onto you.

However, there are some serious downsides to this as well. Think about it: you're on the line if something happens. If for some reason, the business gets into trouble and you end up owing money to someone, *you owe that money*. Not the business, nothing and no one but you. That's a lot of pressure to put on yourself, and you as an individual are very, very vulnerable.

A Limited Liability Company, or LLC, is another option. It's a little more complicated and ends up being a little more expensive in the long run, but it provides a level of protection to you as a person.

If something happens and someone comes after your company for any reason, they are coming after *the company*. Not for yourself. That means your personal assets, like your home, your car, and your belongings, are not on the line. They cannot take them because they are not tied to the business. With a sole-proprietorship, these things are essentially fair game.

Obviously, the extra time setting up an LLC is more than worth it. The protection you give yourself, and your family is absolutely vital.

So, how can I set up an LLC?

Great question! If you're going to go the LLC route – again, I cannot stress enough how important it is to keep yourself safe – there are a few steps and tips I can give you to set yourself on the right path.

The first step you need to take is to go to the Secretary of State's website. You can also go into the office, too, if you so desire – I always prefer to do this kind of thing online.

You need to get the LLC Articles of Organization and fill it out.

Once it's filled out, double-check your state requirements. It's pretty rare, but some states require you to publish an *intent* to form an LLC in a local newspaper. It's a strange and very outdated concept – if you don't absolutely have to, don't waste your money!

Once your LLC Articles of Organization are filled out, you can send your completed form to the Secretary of State's office, along with the fee. This ranges from $100 to $900, depending on your specific state. Do your research on the website, or call your local office to double-check you have everything ready to go.

In a few states, you are going to be asked to pay your corporate taxes immediately. Most, however, let you wait until tax time.

How to Handle Taxes

Speaking of taxes, let's talk about these for a minute. Taxes are no one's favorite part of life, but we all have to handle them at some point.

The first thing you need to do once you've formed your business and gotten started is setting up an EIN or an Employer Identification Number. This identifies you as a unique employer, even if you're the only employee, and tells the IRS who you are.

Head over to the IRS website first, and find your specific state's official tax site through their portal. Fill out everything requested on your state site, and *leave it up*. Do not close this yet.

You're going to be directed back to the IRS main page, where you provide even more information about your business and yourself. Once you fill this out, you will be assigned an EIN. Save this information, and you can close the page.

Return back to the state's page, and fill out the EIN

information requested. Then you can submit everything, and you're done! Keep this number handy; it's important.

After you've taken care of all of the documentation, the IRS needs from you, head over to your state's taxing authority page. Yes, you still need to register with the state as well. I know, it's a lot of steps – I promise it's not that bad!

You need to head over to pay any income taxes that happen when you first create your business and then check with the Department of Revenue – most states require you to apply for a tax seller's permit, which is obviously necessary as, yes, you will probably need to be collecting taxes, depending on how you're selling your products.

With these steps, your taxes are done and taken care of! It seems like a lot to handle, but most of these things are the type of steps you only have to take care of once.

Business Taxes and Other Things You Can't Avoid

Yes, business taxes are a thing. And yes, you're going to need to pay them – I know, I know, it's not a fun subject. I warned you this chapter wasn't fun, just necessary.

Each state is going to handle business taxes a little differently, so be sure to pay attention to your state requirements! While I obviously cannot get into specifics for all 50 states, plus US territories, but I *can* give you an overview, so you're prepared.

No surprise, you're going to be paying income tax on the money that the business makes.

In part, you're going to be filing a Schedule C as part of your tax return. A Schedule C is just an additional form when you fill out the taxes that will help you determine the *net profit* of the company, which is what you are going to be paying on.

Before you do any filings, however, you should look into something called the Qualified Business Income

Deduction. Not every small business qualifies for the QBID, but those that do can get up to 20% off the qualified income for several years. This is *huge* for a business that is just starting out, and these savings can really help you continue to grow your business.

Other Things to Keep in Mind When Starting Your Business

I cannot stress enough how important it is to be legal with the state and local governments. Shockingly, the government does not take well to those who don't follow the law, and nothing will hurt worse than fines or even being shut down because you missed a step, accidentally or not.

Before you start your business, check with your local county – the county you're be working out of and creating in – to see what other registration you might need. Some counties require zero extra steps, while others will ask you to register and even obtain a permit.

Most of the time, only companies that are producing food-grade products like baked goods or candy need inspections and permits, but not always. Every county in the US is a little different, so again, do your research for your specific situation and area. If you have a local business that is similar to your own or a friend who runs a business in your county, feel free to reach out and ask for advice or a starting point. I've found many business owners really do just want to lift each other up and support the community and will be more than willing to help you.

Let's Talk Banking

Banking! Money! Important things that you need to handle before really starting out! Let's dive in.

If you have all your permits in place and your business legal, it's time to think about the bank your LLC is going to use. This can – and maybe even *should* - be different from your personal bank. You should absolutely use a business banking account!

Look around at your local banks for the best fees, rates, and benefits to having a small business account. You will probably find that a relatively local credit union will have the best rates, but be sure to check around at a few different places before you make the final choice. You're looking for a good balance of customer service, interest rates, general fees, and availability. The best bank in the area has awesome rates, but they're open approximately 4 hours a day, and they're 45 minutes away from me – needless to say, I didn't go with them.

Even if you, for some reason, went with a sole-proprietorship and not an LLC, you should always keep your personal and your company money separate. When the lines blur, things get messy.

Do I need a business line of credit?

Most banks are going to offer you a business line of credit. Depending on the age of your business and your capital, this could be only a few hundred dollars or several thousand dollars to start out with. You need to think about it just as you would a personal line of credit.

That means, of course, that you can take it – but be sure you can pay it off at the end of each month and don't carry a balance for too long. Be smart about your spending, and pay close attention to how much you have charged. It will only take one bill you didn't expect from the line of credit to realize you've made a grave error, and putting your business in unnecessary debt isn't something anyone wants to do.

Ultimately, only you know your business's finances, and only you can answer if you *need* one. I like having a business credit card, especially when I was first starting out because I felt that it gave me a little bit of breathing room. If an unexpected expense came out, I didn't always have to scramble and stress about it.

In general, a business credit card is also a better idea than a loan. As you start out, your expenses are going to be relatively small, and you don't really need a huge loan to get by. Always read the fine print, and be sure to find a card that will give you some sort of bonus – rewards, travel miles, or a good APR.

Account, Receipts, and Other Boring Things

No one really likes to talk about accounting (that's why accountants are notoriously the life of the party... ahem), but if you're going to be owning your own business, these are things you're going to have to keep in mind.

Honestly, if you learn anything from this chapter, I want you to take away that keeping **detailed records** is going to save you a lot of time and money in the long run. Seriously, *keep everything* all the time. Get binders, get labels, and keep everything organized.

This doesn't just make filing your taxes at the end of the year a whole lot easier (which I will get into a little in a moment, stay tuned), but it also will help you know where you are financially in your business at all times. This is so incredibly important; I feel like you should always be aware of this – finances are huge, and no matter how much passion or drive you have, if your finances aren't in line, your business *will* fail. Harsh, but a small dose of truth.

Most small businesses use QuickBooks for their basic accounting and tracking. It's not hard to pick up, I promise! Some folks hire a part-time bookkeeper to keep everything organized – that's a fine idea, especially if you're very overwhelmed. You can also hire a bookkeeper to set everything up for you and explain how it works. You don't need to hire someone, though, especially at first if you are trying to save money.

What is a Tax Deduction? What Can I Deduct?

So many small businesses do not take advantage of the tax deductions they can take, and it's such a bummer. It seems like a small amount of money, but it really, really adds up at the end of the year. It also makes a huge difference when we're talking about a small business.

Taking a business meal to talk to a potential vendor? That's a business expense and is tax-deductible. What about traveling to meet with a shirt supplier or to go to an expo? Yep, that's a business expense – and that is tax-deductible.

Home office equipment, like a chair, a desk, a laptop? Yep. Home internet that you use for the business? What about a specific company cell phone or a phone you do business on? Ink, printer, paper, toner... you get the idea, right?

All of these expenses *are* tax deductions, and you need to treat them as such! Save all of your receipts for tax time, and keep them organized and labeled together to save you a serious headache.

Why Do I Need to Pay Self-Employment Taxes?

So many people think that just because they don't have any extra employees, they don't need to pay self-employment taxes. Surprise: while you are a business owner, you are also technically an employee, and as such, you *do* need to pay self-employment taxes. Sorry, that's just the way it works.

These taxes basically pay into social security, as well as Medicare, and they are based on the *net income* of the business itself.

To figure it out, you need to calculate your *estimated taxes* each quarter and pay what you *estimate* you owe. This is basically your business telling the IRS that for the past 3 months, you have made x amount of money and offering the tax amount for that income.

Estimated taxes are generally due in the middle of the month *after* the quarter ends. If the quarter is between September 1 and December 31, the estimated taxes for that quarter are going to be due in the middle of January, on the 15th. If the 15th of January happens to fall on a weekend, taxes are going to be due on the following *business* day. So, if the 15th is a Saturday, they will be due on the 17th, the following Monday.

What If I Just... Don't?

Don't want to calculate taxes every single quarter? Don't want the hassle? Sure, you don't *have* to, but the IRS does not take that attitude lightly.

You will be charged a fine for each quarter that you miss offering estimated taxes for the IRS. This penalty stacks and it also makes the IRS look a little bit closer at what you're doing. Filing your estimated taxes each quarter isn't just because it makes tax time easier in April; it's the law.

Gross Receipt Tax VS State Income Tax

You're probably familiar with the concept of state income tax, but have you ever heard the time *gross receipt tax*? Only a handful of states in the US, like Texas and Nevada, use this term, and its' basically an additional tax on your revenue. This could be in addition to your state income tax, or instead of, depending on the state's laws.

In a few cases, if you have a sole-proprietorship, you won't have to pay this tax. However, I still believe that no matter what state you are in, an LLC is a way to go to protect yourself and the business.

This sounds like a lot to calculate, and I understand you might be overwhelmed, but it's really only hard the *first time* you do it. By the second year of filing taxes, you're going to have all this down, and it won't be stressful at all.

Okay, you might still be a little stressed, but it won't be nearly as bad.

Should I Do My Taxes Myself?!

Here's a big question – can, and should, you do your taxes yourself?

I'm going to go against the grain here and say *absolutely not*. If you haven't picked it up already, I'm all about cutting costs and saving money where you can. There are so many aspects of a small business you can handle yourself, but taxes really aren't one of them.

You don't need an accountant on call at all times, and they don't have to handle every single aspect of your accounting or your bookkeeping. However, business taxes are a whole other beast, and being sure you're doing them right the first time is very, very important.

As previously mentioned, the IRS does not play, and they do not take ignorance as an excuse for filling out the wrong forms, forgetting information, or generally screwing up.

When it comes tax time, I recommend you bring all of your files, receipts, and information to a professional accountant who can help you maximize your deductions and get you paying the appropriate amount for your business. These folks know the tax code very well – it's their job, after all – and they will be able to find you the best deductions and discounts.

It's going to save you both time and money in the long run, and it's a lot less hassle, especially if you do something wrong. I made this mistake one of my first years of owning my own LLC. I thought I could follow directions online and file my own taxes... I ended up missing several things, owing the IRS way too much money, and at the end of it all, I hired a professional *anyway* to fix what mistakes I made. The fix cost more than it would have to hire them in the first place.

Not my proudest moment, but you can learn from me.

Upfront Costs + Pricing Your Product to Make Money

You're a business; you're not a charity. Therefore, you need to make sure you are making money on each product that you sell, *in general*. There are some small exceptions, like how a grocery store has 'loss leaders' (Costco's $4.99

chickens come to mind), but in general... you're here to provide a product and *make money* for your time.

That is why pricing is so important.

The Michael Scott Lesson in Proper Pricing

Have you seen the hit NBC show *The Office*? Yes, I'm putting a Michael Scott reference – if you have seen this plot line in the 5th season, you know where I'm going with this, but bear with me for a moment. This really is an excellent example of poor pricing strategies.

After dealing with Jan and Ryan's awful replacement, Charles Miner, Michael decides he is going to go nuclear – he will quit his position as Regional Manager of Dunder Mifflin Scranton and start his own company. *The Michael Scott Paper Company*. Pam quits too, and the duo picks up Ryan Howard, former intern and blue-collar criminal, to run the business.

They work out of what really amounts to a closet, but they pick up a handful of clients, mostly taken from Dunder

Mifflin using Michael's connections before they meet with an accountant and make a terrible discovery: Ryan has no idea how to price paper properly, or anything really, and they are losing money at a rapid pace. The more customers they get, in fact, they are going to lose more money.

They can't afford a delivery driver, a bigger office, or even new equipment. Despite Ryan's "business degree," they did not take into account salaries or any overhead costs.

The company ended up being bought out by David Wallace and Dunder Mifflin, but that was sheer luck: Michael could have easily gone bankrupt.

What We Learn From This

Pricing isn't quite as easy as it might seem, and you need to be sure you are taking into account *everything* when you're setting a price for your t-shirts. You're not just trying to make back the money it cost to create that shirt, but every expense (in a small part) that led to that point.

Ultimately, only *you* know how much you are spending,

but I'm going to try and help give you a generalized idea so you can get the right start on it. Only you know the right amounts for your own business. Remember that statement when someone gives you a hard time about your pricing, by the way – it's bound to happen!

Remember that you are always allowed to raise prices if you accidentally hit the Michael Scott level of mistakes. If you look at the numbers and it's simply *not working out*, how much can you raise prices to help that? Of course, I always recommend looking at other costs to cut first, but you don't owe anyone anything. You can't get more money from customers that have already purchased your products, but you can fix your mistakes going forward.

There Are Like 800 Things to Consider in Pricing

Alright, alright, I'm being dramatic again – but there are a lot of things to consider when you are thinking about the selling price for your t-shirts. You need to think about the raw cost of materials *as well as* costs like marketing, packaging, and even just your overhead.

Every single time you sell a shirt, you need to recoup all of these costs, bottom line. If you are not, you're not making money and setting yourself up to fail.

You also need to think about one of the most important costs: yourself! You need to calculate a fair hourly wage for the work you put into the t-shirt. Even if you don't feel like you need to pay yourself (which, come on. Everyone needs some type of income), you will *someday* have to pay *someone* to create these shirts when you scale up... that's the dream, right? This cost needs to be built into the price, or you are never going to be able to scale your business to higher levels.

For a very, very simple breakdown, consider this formula, which is the starting point for many small business pricing models.

The Single Unit Cost = Cost of One Batch / The Total Number of Units in the Batch

Let's break it down a little more.

The cost of the batch is how much it costs to make a set of

shirts. If you make 10 shirts in a batch at a time, that is your total number of units in the batch. If it costs you $100, including the raw materials, to make that batch, then the *single unit* cost is going to be $10. That is your starting cost. This is *not* the cost that you are selling your t-shirts at, though.

Your selling cost obviously needs to be *higher*. If your unit cost is $10 and you sell it for $20, you are making $10 in profit per shirt. That makes sense, right?

So How Much Profit?

There are a few ways they teach you in business school when you start learning about pricing strategies. I'm going to touch on the most common ones – you can go through these all and find which one appeals to you most and fits with your ideal business strategy. Again, I'm not here to necessarily tell you what is right and what is wrong for your specific business! I'm just here to give you some options.

The **fixed price strategy** is absolutely the simplest pricing strategy around, and it's what many new businesses first start off with just because it's so easy to calculate. If you have a set, a fixed amount of money you want or need to make each month, you simply build that into your price.

If you're selling 100 t-shirts each month, and you want to make, say, $600 a month in profit, you need to add $6 to every t-shirt you make.

Simple, right? This is why it appeals to so many new business owners. You don't *really* have to think about your pricing too much. The downside, however, is that it is hard to grow with this strategy. There isn't a lot of flexibility.

The **multiplier strategy** is a little more complex and involves math, but it does have a lot of benefits. With the multiplier strategy, you will always make a set amount of profit *no matter* what your product is or how many you are selling. When you're looking at your final cost, you will be looking at the unit cost (which we figured out above – in the example, it is $10) and multiplying it. The name makes sense, right?

Okay, so if you want to sell your product for 2x what it costs you, and your shirt costs $10 to make, you will be selling it for $20. If you want to sell your product for 1.5x the amount it costs you, each shirt will sell for $15.

There's one more strategy – the **percentage strategy**. This is very, very similar to the above strategy, but as the name suggests, it works with percentages, not straight multiplication.

So, if you want to sell your t-shirts for 50% more than what they cost you, you're going to calculate what 50% of the unit price is and add that on. For a $10 shirt, that is $15. If you want to sell for 65% more, you'll be selling for $16.50.

Something important to think about when you're calculating your sale price and your pricing strategy is your target market. If you are selling t-shirts with fun phrases and graphics to college kids, they're probably not going to be able to afford $35 shirts. A mom with 2 kids who feels guilty about grabbing coffee once a week isn't to drop a ton of cash on your shirts.

Put a lot of thought into *who* your target market is and what they can afford, as well as what they would be willing to *pay*.

Where Does Wholesale Fit in?

Wholesale pricing is a little different because it's more complicated. You're not selling directly to consumers, and you're instead selling to a company or brand that will turn around and make an additional profit on it.

Therefore, you cannot have your wholesale pricing be the same as your retail pricing.

You might be asking yourself, *why would anyone sell for less?* That's a fair point of view, but there are some serious upsides to wholesale. For one, you have a guaranteed sale amount. You may be selling for a smaller profit overall, but if you have 50, 100, or 300 promised purchases, that is a big deal. You also don't have to handle marketing for all of those shirts, managing that inventory, shipping individually... there are certainly upsides.

Find a price for your products that are lower than your standard retail but have enough wiggle room to make selling them worth it for you. Be aware that the upsides to wholesale aren't always worth it for everyone, and it's okay to step away from a wholesale deal if you aren't making enough profit to make it worth it *for you*.

What Can I Expect to Pay Upfront?

The upfront costs for building your t-shirt business vary wildly depending on how you want to start if you're handling your own inventory, where you're going to be working... there are thousands of variables. I'm going to help you get an idea of the expense you *could* be occurring as you start this journey and to think about the money you're going to need upfront.

Inventory + Supplies

If you're going to be using a print-on-demand service, this isn't going to apply to you – but if you will be creating your own shirts and managing your own inventory, this is going to be your biggest *reoccurring* expense.

Finding a good supplier of **quality, inexpensive** shirts is going to be your biggest expense. You may have to order from a few different places before you find what you're really looking for. Be sure you're choosing both a shirt *you* like to work with and that works well with whatever process you're using. Sometimes shirts can look great plain, but when you place a vinyl graphic over them, it changes the whole look.

You also need to be sure you're taking into account how much the final product will cost to the consumer. You may find amazing shirts that look incredible, but if they are very expensive and your target market *doesn't* spend a ton on clothing... well, you're going to have a big issue.

Your next major reoccurring expense is going to be the **materials** to make your design. Whether you're choosing screenprinting, painting, bleaching, or vinyl, you are going to need to continually purchase your materials as you grow and create more shirts.

Just like with shirts, finding a quality supplier is crucial. You simply cannot afford to keep buying your supplies at a local craft store in a home-craft quality. Look for a wholesaler that will sell you supplies in a quantity that works for *you*. You might not be able to afford, or realistically store, several month's worth of supplies, especially when you're starting out. *That's okay.* You don't have to spend $5k on supplies right up front. Purchase the quantities you can afford, and you can store.

Overhead is a huge expense that so many people underestimate. I want you to think about where you're going to be creating and storing your shirts. Are you able to create in a space you already have, like a garage, a finished basement, or an extra spare room? Can you ask family or good friends to donate space in a shed or garage so you don't have to rent a space?

These should be your first options. So many businesses set themselves up for failure because they're spending too much money on the things they don't have to. If you can get a space for free or very cheap, you should jump on it — at least at first! I heavily encourage you to not spend money you don't have to, especially when you're first building your business. It sounds cool and fun to have your own space in a building, of course, but if you can't afford it... is it worth it?

If you don't have realistic or affordable options that don't involve cash, you're going to need to find a space to rent – or purchase, I suppose – to work out of. Finding a space that works for you can be a challenge, so be patient. Don't jump at the first opportunity you get if it's not right for you just because it is immediate.

If you're looking for just a workspace, start with business listings – a different type of listing from a normal retail listing. I've found some amazing starter spaces in, believe it or not, storage spaces. They're not just empty boxes – many larger storage facilities have workspaces you can rent by the month. Look for a space big enough to fit any equipment you're going to be using and that can store all of your inventory – both the finished products and the inks, dyes, pieces of vinyl, etc., that you're going to be using.

Be sure you have a climate-controlled unit if you live anywhere in the world that either gets cold *or* warm, and electricity is a must. Battery-operated anything just doesn't cut it when it comes to creating your product or your workspace.

There are additional **overhead** expenses that could be occurring, as well, and you need to be sure to consider that. Even if you're working out of your garage or your basement, your electricity bills are going to go up, as well as water, heat... you're going to be spending a lot more time in that space.

If you're renting a space, be sure you know if you'll be charged for any additional expenses or utilities. These small expenses add up, and they can sink even the best-intentioned business.

Insurance is a big expense that so many new business owners don't think about, but you *need business insurance*. If something happens and your workspace goes up in flames, you lose all your product. That's awful, and I wouldn't wish that on my worst enemy, but it can happen. Business insurance can keep you safe from that, financially – plus cover you in many other ways.

What additional **equipment** are you going to need in order to be successful? Obviously, you don't have to blow thousands of dollars for screen printing equipment, but there may be equipment you're going to need in order to keep up with demand. Make sure you properly price *everything* so you know your actual costs, not just what you saw on a single eBay listing or on an old Facebook Marketplace listing.

Creating an **online platform** is going to be an expense, which is covered more in another section, but it's also something you need to keep in mind. Host fees, online seller fees, and the fees that are taken on top of your payments are all small expenses that can add up in a big way.

Marketing is a hidden expense you might not think about as well. Setting up your online presence and running ads is a big way to get new business and reach your target market, but it certainly isn't free. Again, these fees and how to do it are all in the marketing section of this book, but it's important that you remember that expense.

Packaging is going to be another one of those expenses you might not think about immediately. What are you going to put into the box if you're shipping your shirts? Are you going to put a card in there? That's an expense. A custom label? That's an expense.

How are you going to package your shirts? What will they ship in? Are you going to spend the extra money on custom boxes or packages to make yourself stand out when it gets delivered, or are you going to save that shipping cost and transfer the money to another aspect of your business?

Obviously, the only right answer is the one that fits into your business, your budget, and maybe most importantly, your target market. Will your target market value a lux packaging style? Do they care if it comes in a USPS puffy bag? What image are you selling? Your packaging should fit with your brand and your target market.

Do I Need Cushion: A Lesson

When you've gathered all of these expenses up, you're going to have a good base idea of what your actual, real startup costs are going to be. So many businesses make the mistake of cutting their money so close that they can only cover these expenses.

But what if something happens in your first few weeks? What if something breaks, and you need to replace a piece of equipment? What if something goes haywire and you ruin a whole stack of shirts? You're going to need the money to replace them and keep yourself going.

It's imperative that you have a financial cushion and some serious wiggle room. You never want to be caught in a situation where you literally don't have the money for something, and production stops because of that.

While you can rely on a business line of credit for some things, having a liquid cash cushion is going to be a big deal. Don't cut it so close that you can't manage the surprise expenses, or you're going to sink your business without even realizing it.

Harsh, but true.

Should You Get Investor Funding?

Here's a big question – should you bring on an investor to help you with your startup costs? After all, there's a good chance you're not Tesla or Google, and you probably don't have a ton of cash to keep throwing at your business.

Depending on how high startup costs are, after all, it can take a small business between two and three *years* to start seeing any real profit. Depending on how expensive your business is to start, if you're going to have a storefront, and if you'll need employees for that storefront (I'm going to talk about that in the next section!), your margins might be *very tight* for a while.

There are a few things you need to think about, questions you need to ask yourself – and the business – and decisions you need to make before you pull in anyone else for funding.

First, you need to determine *how much funding you need.* This is really important! You need to know what you're asking for... just asking for "money" or "an investment" isn't going to get you anywhere. Remember, if you need a lot of capital, you can secure it from multiple places.

The most common way businesses get capital is a small business loan, where you pay interest on the loan in exchange for the money upfront. Once your loan ends, your business is still yours – this is a big benefit. This isn't really an investor, but the topic gets confused, so it's worth mentioning. If you want to retain 100% control and ownership of your business, but you need some startup cash, this is probably the best way to go about it.

What About SBA-Guarantee?

If you're in the US, there's something called an SBA-Guaranteed loan. Some banks will not offer loans for smaller startup businesses because there is so much risk, and so many people want a loan. If you're struggling to secure a traditional business loan, this is a great option for you.

It basically means that the U.S. Small Business Administration (SBA) has agreed to be a guarantor for you. If something happens and your default on your loan, the bank is covered financially by the government. You can go to the SBA's website directly and see if your business could potentially qualify. They also offer surety bonds, disaster assistance and can help you find an investor should you go that route. Honestly, the SBA has some great assistance for small businesses and isn't utilized enough.

If you're approaching an individual or an investment firm, you're going to need a few things. A good business **plan** – the traditional kind! - is a must. I recommend tailoring your business plan specifically to the individual you're looking to get an investment from, and include everything you plan to do with their money, as well as exactly how much you're asking of them.

The more specifically you lay out your needs for the money, the more likely someone is to invest. Most people like to know what their money is going to, after all. If you feel you need a liquid cash cushion, I don't recommend marking your investors' money for that. You can use the money you're putting into the business for that and use your investors' money to directly, immediately influence the business.

You need to realize when you're approaching a company or an individual for funding, you're *not* asking for a loan. What you're doing is offering *equity* in exchange for financing, or sometimes a combination of equity *and* a loan.

It's just like Shark Tank (which, if you've never watched it before, I recommend at least one episode to get a feel for some common questions you might be asked... it may be a TV show, but there are real discussions happening.

Some episodes, of course, are better or more realistic than others), where an investor will offer you x amount of money for y amount of ownership.

Generally, there are two types of partners – silent and active. A silent investor is just that, silent. They have invested money in your company, they own a portion of it, but they trust you to handle the business management and arrangements and simply receive a portion of the profits or hold ownership.

Often, an investor will loan you (a made-up example!) $10,000 and ask to be paid back within 5 years, along with owning 10% of your company.

An active investor, however, is more involved in the day-to-day and big picture of the company. You can think of this investor as more like a partner. They may own less of the company than you (they should, in fact!), but they want to be involved and participate in operations, money management, and more. If you're concerned about jumping into a business alone, you're looking for sage advice, or just don't want everything on your shoulders, this type of investor is a huge asset.

However, it's important to remember you may not always agree with your partner. You need to establish before investment happens who has the final say on what issues.

Be Careful of Giving Up *Too* Much

Here's the deal – it's really, really tempting to give up more of your business in exchange for cash, especially when you're strapped or you're getting many smaller investments. 5% here, 10% here, all you can see is your business growing and your ability to reach more people and do more things expanding.

However, the more of your business you give up, the less it is *your* business. Be very careful and strategic if and when you give up a portion of your business. You really never want to hold less than 51% of your business.

The Sharks on Shark Tank always say it's better to have a small slice of a big pie than all of a tiny pie, and they're not *wrong*, but don't give up so much of your business it's no longer *your business*, but you're simply working for a company.

Expanding 101: Opening a Storefront, Hiring Help, and Expanding Your Product Line

So you want to open a storefront, in order to sell your t-shirts in person.

That's awesome! This is a big step, and I congratulate you. I will say that maintaining an online storefront in conjunction with your in-person storefront is a great idea, but I can't make you do that, obviously.

If you're thinking about opening a shop, there are some things you need to consider. All of this is going to depend on where you live and what exactly you're selling, obviously, but I can help guide you in the right direction!

The Cost Involved

Most businesses don't own their property; they lease it. While you can absolutely *outright buy* a building to work out of and sell your things, this is a big expense up front, and most small business owners just don't have that kind of capital, even with loans and investor funding.

Instead, leasing a storefront is probably going to be your best bet. But the lease amount isn't the only amount you're going to be paying.

In addition to finding a space that is for you, you're going to need to outfit the entire space. Most business rentals

167

provide you with the *absolute basics*, which are a floor, a ceiling, and some lights. You need to put up shelves, a counter for checking out, maybe a changing room if you want your customers to be able to try on your merchandise. You also want to make it look appealing – this could mean that you need to put down floors, paint walls, or put up framed pictures, wallpaper, and more.

These expenses *add up* and fast. You need to make sure you have the capital to fully outfit your building, or you'll turn off potential customers.

You are also going to need to pay to keep the electricity on. You will have to heat your facility in the winter and run your AC during the summer. If you have plumbing (which, I hope so – nothing is worse than working a long shift without access to a bathroom), you're going to need water. You will also need internet, if for no other reason than to take payment and reorder inventory, and a phone line is very important for a physical store so customers can call to see if you're open, check your hours, or ask about current inventory.

Before you sign a lease, you also need to carefully check

what is included. Some buildings will run more like an apartment rental, where maintenance is included. Others *do not.* My husband's family runs a business, and they are responsible for all repairs and maintenance to the building, despite not owning it... a few years ago, a bad storm came through and completely flooded the conference room, and they were on the hook not just for fixing the roof, but they had to work with their insurance to cover the damage on the inside, including a completely destroyed conference table, ripping up the carpet, and replacing some of the wiring in the ceiling.

Who pays for lawn care? Is it handled by the owner, or are you expected to bring out a lawnmower every week? Are you supposed to pay property tax? Yes, some leasing companies ask you to *pay the property tax*, even though you don't own the property itself. Be sure you read your contract thoroughly, and ask these questions.

Know what you're signing onto *before* you sign on the dotted line.

Finding The Perfect Spot

It's so, so important you have a good location for your shop before you pick out a place. The right location will absolutely make or break your storefront, and there's nothing worse than knowing you've got a great product at a great price point but not being able to sell it because no one is walking through the door.

The first question you need to ask yourself is, *where does your target market shop*? Is it a mall (though, does anyone shop at the mall anymore?)? Is it on or near a college campus? What neighborhoods do you think your target market lives in, and what areas are they willing to travel to?

You might sell the best merchandise possible, but if your target market isn't shopping in that area, you're not going to be very successful. At least, you'll never reach your potential!

After you have the areas narrowed down, look at the properties themselves. Is there foot traffic? Are there other successful shops nearby that will help bring in customers? Surrounding yourself with busy businesses means there is more traffic to the area overall, which will help increase those who notice you and stop in 'just to look.' In short, if your business is already on its path – coming home from work, going to the grocery store, going to another retail location – your customers are more likely to stop in.

What *are* the other businesses in the area? Are you setting yourself up against stiff competition, or are you the only store with this specific type of product within a reasonable driving distance? You shouldn't set up shop next to an established competitor unless you really have something they don't have. Even if your product is fundamentally better, you're going to struggle to pull loyal customers away.

How much work does the building itself need? What all are you going to have to do in order to open shop, and how much is that going to cost you? It might be worth doing a walk-through with a contractor or pricing certain things like shelving units and counters *before* you pull the trigger. Nothing worse than signing the lease *before* finding out that it's going to be an additional few thousand dollars you weren't expecting to open the doors.

Is it *enough* space? Is it too much? Yes, too much is a real thing – if you've ever walked into a store and been immediately uncomfortable because the room was simply too large for what it was holding, you know exactly what I'm talking about. Few things are more awkward for a shopper. While you don't want to jam-pack your store and make it awkward to walk around in, you do want to try and find a nice balance.

Is there space in the back, too? Do you have room to create new shirts or store the shirts you have already created? If it doesn't have that space, can you *create* the space by placing a wall and a door to a back room?

What's the parking situation like? From personal experience, I can tell you, if I know a business has an awful parking lot, I'm *not* going in. There is a small storefront on a busy main road I pass probably four times a week. Each time I think it's a store I would legitimately love to shop in... but their parking lot is *tiny*, with maybe 7 spots tucked in next to the building and almost no room to maneuver. I've never been in because it's just way too much hassle.

Most folks say 5-8 spaces of parking per 1,000 square feet of storefront, but I think having a few extra spots is a good idea, too.

What are the zoning regulations in the area? What about signage rules? Some counties or even *streets* have specifics rules on the signage you're allowed to put up or the way you advertise your business. Be sure you know what you can do in the area *legally*, so people know where you are.

Finally, think about the shop in terms of your personal life. Do you have to drive 5 minutes to open the shop every morning, or is it more like 45? If you have a long commute, it can be incredibly draining – and for many, make the idea of being your own boss a lot less appealing. Don't underestimate how soul-crushing a long commute is day in and day out, especially if you're going to be in traffic.

A Mall/Shopping Plaza Versus a Downtown Location Versus Standalone

Just like so many other aspects of small business ownership, there is no right or wrong answer here. I'm going to present the pros and cons of all of these, and you can decide what is right for your business in your town. Every city in the US is going to be a little bit different, so you need to approach this issue with an open mind.

You may also have a vision of what your perfect business storefront looks like, and you don't need this section. I still think reading through and considering the benefits of all is smart.

A Mall, or a Shopping Center

Malls have been a US staple for a long time, with shopping plazas not far behind. How many can say that they don't go to one or the other at least once a week for a variety of needs, like groceries, a Target run, or just to shop?

There are a few major benefits for these storefront

locations! The biggest one is the foot traffic you are going to get. Even if someone is not coming to the plaza or the mall specifically for your business, they may stop in just because you're there. That can lead to a bonus sale.

Customers also look to these locations specifically when they want to purchase something. You go to the mall to *buy something*, after all.

You also rarely have to worry about parking in these locations because the mall *or* the plaza was specifically designed to hold a reasonable number of cars.

The downsides, however, do exist. Many malls in America are on their way out, and choosing a location in a 'dead' mall is a recipe for disaster. Traffic for many of these malls will not return, and you need to be aware that going this route is a huge risk.

You also often have a lot of competition, depending on the plaza or mall you choose. I mentioned above how dangerous it can be to move into a location that is too close to a direct competitor.

A Downtown Location

Thinking about a downtown storefront?! That's a great idea! There are a lot of benefits to finding a building downtown to set up shop in.

The biggest one is the increased foot traffic! It's not generally just one type of customer that is going to be walking around downtown checking out shops, and you have a chance to reach a wide audience. Depending on your target market and the designs you create, this can be a huge win.

If your area is going through a revitalization, as many downtown areas have been in the last 10-15 years, this could be a great opportunity to get in on the ground floor or take advantage of that. You are also helping your community, and many downtown storefronts are at the heart of that effort.

There are some downsides, though. Parking is a huge concern for many downtown locations! Minimal street parking and no public parking lots means your customers will have to really struggle to visit you, and this can scare away a lot of new potential customers.

If there are many similar stores downtown, you're going to be fighting a tough fight.

In addition, if your downtown area is mostly offices or businesses, you are seriously restricting your customer base. Think about not just how much traffic the area gets but *what kind* of traffic.

A Standalone Storefront

Sometimes the most appealing option for new businesses, a standalone storefront, can be a real asset. Generally speaking, these locations have a minimal number of rules and regulations. At a mall store I once had, I was not allowed to put up a ladder while the mall was open... it doesn't matter if I had customers in the store or not. With a standalone store, you never really face these issues.

You also generally have a great amount of parking, and it's all for you and your customers. Having a large parking lot or a big lot is great.

Traffic, however, can be harder to judge and more unpredictable. After all, customers need to pull into your lot *just for you*. Marketing and signage costs often go up in these locations.

Additionally, there are often other expenses associated with these locations. Many landlords expect you to handle lawn care and maintenance, though that is not *always* the case. Zoning laws are also sometimes confusing or hard to determine, so you need to be extra clear in what you can and cannot have on your property.

When To Hire Help

Here's another question new businesses really struggle with: when should you hire help, and where should you find them?

It's hard to admit for some, but you are not a one-person army. As your business grows and expands, you may be put into a situation where you are limited not by your customers or your sales but by your own ability to create and sell your t-shirts.

There are a few questions you need to answer when you're thinking of hiring help.

Can I meet demand on my own?

This is the biggest question. Are you able to meet the demand for your products on your own without hiring anyone? Do you find yourself marking things out of stock, running out of product, or running late on fulfilling orders because you simply can't catch up?

Is production now taking away from other duties?

When you start, you might not struggle to balance marketing, bookkeeping, website maintenance, and customer service with production. It's a lot, sure, but you can handle it.

However, as you grow, you may find yourself overwhelmed. Is the raw production of the shirts taking up all of your time? Are you spending so much time creating shirts that have sold, or are selling, that you can't respond to customer inquiries in a timely fashion? Are you neglecting marketing? Are you neglecting growth opportunities simply because you do not have time in the day for everything?

If the answer is yes, this is a big red flag – and it may be time to bring someone else on board.

Can I afford it? If not, why?

Can you *actually* afford to pay another person for work? Is it in the budget? Are you making enough profit that another hourly worker isn't going to kill your finances and leave you in debt? While there are no certainties in life, you should be looking at your financial projections and your past sales to determine that.

Remember that by hiring someone else, you are freeing yourself up from duty – and often, that time can be put back into the business to continue to grow.

If you cannot afford to bring someone on, but you need the extra hands, you should be asking yourself why. Are your expenses too high? Are your profit margins too low? I'm not saying that your small business should be able to realistically pay a $60k with benefits salary, but if you can't hire a worker for a few hours a day or a week while you are making money and are overwhelmed, you need to reassess what is happening with your business.

I cannot stress enough to *hire smart*, not blindly. So many, and I mean *so many* small businesses hire someone because they are friends, they are family, they came recommended... *whatever*. These people are often not qualified for the position they find themselves in, and that can hurt the growth of the business.

Give yourself the best possible chance at success by hiring a *qualified* candidate, even if it ruffles some feathers.

Hiring smart is two-part, though – you should also be strategic in what positions you hire *for*. Know what your weak spots are, and hire to strengthen your business. If you are a year into your business and you know bookkeeping is something you dread, hire a bookkeeper. You will feel better knowing it is taken care of, and you can focus that time back into the business – you're happier, and your business will continue to prosper.

If you know, you hate marketing, or you feel clueless, feel

free to find a freelance marketing specialist for a few hours a month to help run ad campaigns and give you marketing advice. That whatever you hate, or you feel like you are not good enough at, off of your plate to give you more room to grow.

If you *enjoy* working behind the counter at your store, set yourself up so that you can still do that. If you love the hands-on technique of creating your shirts, *do that*. Set yourself up so you're hiring *smart* and you can continue to do what you love while being involved in the business.

Expanding Your Product Line: Be Careful

Expansion is super important! It's really hard to grow your business when you're only selling the same handful of items... if you don't update your store, update your designs, and update your merchandise, you're going to really struggle.

Be smart in the amount of product you carry – never overwhelm yourself or your store – but you want to keep some variety. Only carry as much as you can reasonably produce in a given time, obviously. You don't want to have so many designs, so many prints, that you can't keep up and get lost in the shuffle.

When you're considering branching out, think about what your target market likes. I know, I say this a thousand times, and you're probably tired of hearing it – but it's so, so true. Does your target market spend a lot of time outdoors? Maybe a water bottle with some of your signature designs. Are they always on the run? A to-go coffee cup with their favorite design would be a great addition. Sweaters, hoodies, and jackets are all easy options to branch out and expand your line.

Tote bags are also a great choice, and the same printing techniques you use for your shirts will often transfer over.

Mugs and drinkware are another branching addition you can add to your store. Stickers are a high-profit item that customers will often 'impulse buy,' and you can use the existing designs you have.

If you have 35 pages of product for your clients to sift through online, there's a real chance they just get overwhelmed and leave your store. Keeping things organized, however, can help this some.

If you're not sure how to work on expanding, as always, I'm going to recommend you take a look at a competitor. What are they selling? How many different *types* of items do they have, and how many times are they just reusing a single design? This is going to give you a good indicator of what things your target market likes and is buying and creates a good jumping point for you.

Don't be afraid to try new things and branch out. That is how you expand, reach more people, and generate more sales!

Social Media, Marketing, and How to Gain + Keep Customers

Marketing is, needless to say, incredibly important! Your target market is really going to determine the specifics of your marketing plan (you *have* read that section, right? You have determined your target market, and you understand why it is important?), but you *don't* need a degree in marketing from a top university in order to run a successful marketing campaign.

Using social media and the tools available to you, along with some time and effort, you can formulate a solid marketing plan and gain new customers. Don't let marketing be intimidating – let's take it one step at a time, and I will break it down for you so you can tackle your own marketing.

Do I Have To?

Well, no. You don't have to handle your own marketing – but you *do* need marketing in order to grow your business. If you don't advertise and share yourself, how will anyone know you exist?!

Just like you might hire a freelancer to build your website, you can hire a freelancer to do your marketing and social media for you. However, especially when starting out, this is an expense that isn't strictly necessary. You *absolutely* can handle your own marketing.

If you have gotten to a point where you feel that you need to hire it out, there's no shame in asking for help. But I do think you should approach it by yourself first if only to understand the amount of work involved in crafting a marketing plan and setting it up. Having a good idea of how it all works also will give you a better idea of how to handle hiring someone else to handle it, too.

Why You Need Social Media

I get it, social media is a cancer in society, and it's bringing you down. Studies have shown that scrolling mindlessly through Facebook, Instagram, or other social media accounts is really just *a bummer*. (Not a scientific term) However, social media is probably where most of your target market is, too.

Nearly 4 *billion* people use different social media platforms. Over 55% of the entire world's population is on social media, with 82% of those 13 and older in North America. Seriously, it's a lot.

Despite all the issues the platform has had over the years, Facebook is still the leader, with 68% of adults saying they used the platform regularly (as of 2018). The average person spends over 2 hours on social media each day as of early 2021.

Can you understand yet why I'm telling you this?

In general, social media is going to be the best way to reach your audience. Unless, for some reason, you're selling to folks without a computer (what a target market, honestly), social media is going to play a huge role in gathering customers and keeping them.

No matter how you *personally* feel about social media... yes. You need social media if you really want to be successful in your business. I'm sorry if that's a bummer for you, but it's true!

How Often Should I Be Posting?

This really is a hard question to answer. Once you have established your brand and your store is up and running, you are probably asking, *how often should I be posting on social media?*

The answer is going to depend truly on how much time you have to dedicate to your new business and how aggressively you want to market, but I am going to suggest *at least* once a day. For platforms like Instagram and Facebook, you should also post one to two times a day on your stories. These are a great way to reach casual viewers, who really just log into social media to check in on stories and lightly browse.

Don't Ignore Them, Though

You should, however, be *checking* your social media platforms each day! Customers often use social media to communicate issues, ask questions, and just interact with you. You are a small business, and you should encourage people to continue to think of you not just as a faceless corporation but as a *person* running a *business*. People love supporting actual members of a community!

Always interact with people posting on your social media. This is how you *keep* customers! I recommend dedicating myself to checking social media twice a day – once in the morning and once at night. Check your messages, respond to any comments on posts, and answer questions anyone has.

What Do I Even Post?!

Posting once a day might seem like a lot to you, but you don't need to go in every single day to make these posts! Most social media platforms have built-in schedulers, so if you spend an hour or two once a week, you can schedule posts for every single day of the week. This makes it *very* easy to appear super active on these platforms without dedicating hours a day.

If you're struggling on how to figure what to post, and you're struggling to come up with content, consider taking a look at your competitor's social media! While I would *never* suggest you outright steal their posts, browsing for inspiration and ideas is totally acceptable!

When you're thinking about crafting posts, think *seasonally*, and think about what is going on. Is it summer? A fun post with lemonade, picnics, and your best summer designs is great. Is it fall? Think pumpkins, cornstalks, etc. Have fun with it!

Don't be afraid to post engaging content, too. Add polls, start discussions, ask questions of your customers or potential customers! If you start a discussion and people participate, they are thinking more about your brand, which can translate to sales.

Be Sure Your Social Media Matches Your Brand

After you make your profiles and before you run any advertisements, ask yourself: does this match my brand? Will everything appeal to my target market? Does my header image make sense? Does my profile image make sense?

You should go back to this question every few months and make sure your social media accounts are on track. You can also ask yourself if your *posts* are on-brand. Does everything fit your image? Your brand? Your desired look? If the answer is no, or even just 'maybe,' you need to reevaluate what is wrong and figure out how to get yourself back on your brand.

Facebook Advertising

Facebook makes advertising on their platform *incredibly*

easy, which can be dangerous, honestly – a trap many new businesses fall into is putting out way too many ads and accidentally spend a ton of money without realizing it. Be sure to advertise *thoughtfully* and *carefully*.

If you haven't set up a business social media account, that should be your first step. Facebook makes it very easy to set up your business page *and* attach it to your personal page, so checking your notifications and monitoring your progress isn't hard at all.

Once you have everything up and running, when you are on your business page, all you have to do is select the *Promote* icon on a post. Setting up the advertising campaign is just a few buttons – select how long you want it to run for, the audience you wish to target, and Facebook will do the rest, showing your posts to those that fit in your ideal demographic.

Targeting a *demographic* like this is a great way to really get in with your target market and really focus on the people most likely to purchase your products. *As always*, the closer you get to speaking with your target market, the better off you are.

What Posts Do Best?

When you are promoting a post on social media, in general, video posts perform better than just pictures. This is for a few reasons, including videos are really just more eye-catching. Videos will often cause a person to pause to 'see what happens, which really is the goal.

Doing a video is certainly a technical step up, though – if you are not ready for that step, you should work on promoting your best picture posts.

You should also reduce the *frequency* of your promoted posts and instead focus on quality. Your target market doesn't want to see your posts 4 or 5 times a day, after all!

Once you get a few ads out there, I encourage you to experiment some – do some a/b testing! See what your target market likes best and responds to. You're going to know within a few days if a campaign you're running is successful or not, and you can focus on the successful elements in the future.

Facebook Data

Facebook will collect a *ton* of useful data for you when you're working on your marketing and setting everything up, but you need to know how to use it. As of June 2021, Facebook Analytics has officially gone away. However, Facebook has a few other options – this isn't the end of data collection.

Facebook Business Suite is what the platform recommends businesses switch to. This platform gives users a top-down look at not only their Facebook business page but their Instagram page as well, and you can manage all of your marketing and advertising on both platforms.

Facebook Business Suite also has the Insights section, which allows you to see metrics and trends. These include things like the demographics of your current followers (so you know if you're reaching your target market!), the reach of your page (how many people are seeing your posts, anyway?), and the engagement levels, including likes and comments on what you post.

You Can Also Use Outside Platforms

If you hate Facebook's interface (which I get), you can use outside tools to look at your metrics and manage your data. The more data you have, the better off you are – I cannot stress this enough.

Hootsuite Analytics will cover all of your social media platforms, and you can break down each post for reach, shares, clicks, comments, etc. It's a great tool.

Mobile Matters

This *does not* just apply to Facebook but all social media platforms. Something many new business owners don't think about is how mobile users are going to see their posts. However, the *vast majority* of social media users are using, you guessed it, their phones! Think about when *you* scroll through Facebook or Instagram… is it lying in bed? Standing in line? At lunch, while you're munching on chips?

For most people, it is!

Making sure your posts are friendly for mobile users! Easy to scroll, easy to read, and not so large, they're hard to get past.

Instagram Ads

Running ads on Instagram is actually very similar to Facebook – no surprise, I suppose, considering they are owned by the same folks. If you're thinking you should *only* run ads on Facebook and ignore Instagram, I'm going to stop you there.

The Instagram app is one of the most downloaded apps *ever*, and so many people utilize Instagram across a wide variety of demographics and for many reasons. Again, there is a good chance your target market uses the platform, and you should, too.

Just like with Facebook, you should have a business Instagram account that you post to regularly – at least once a day, with at least one story a day as well. With Instagram, however, a big difference is that you cannot post a link when you make a post. Instead, you need to "drop the link" in your bio.

You can link to your shop in your Instagram bio, but you can also use a link in bio tool like Tap.bio, Linktree, or Lnk.bio. These online services basically let you attach individual links to different posts, so when a user clicks on your Linktree link, for example, they can see all the pictures that you have posted and click on associated links of products.

When you promote a post, it's a similar process as Facebook. You can target your specific market, choose how long it runs, and who sees it. Be sure you're carefully choosing your target market only (don't waste money advertising to someone who isn't interested in your product), and choose only your best-written, best-constructed posts to advertise with.

You should be thoughtful and careful instead of doing the shotgun approach of throwing it all against the wall and seeing what sticks.

#Hashtag

With Instagram more than Facebook, hashtags are *very* important. If you're a regular Instagram user, you probably know that, though – hashtags are how you find similar-minded people, find posts on topics that interest you, and more.

When you're thinking about how many hashtags to use, I suggest *be generous* but don't go overboard. Most marketing experts recommend between 7 and 30, which feels aggressive to me. I personally use between 5 and 20, depending on the topic.

If you're trying to figure out what hashtags to use, you can open Instagram up on your desktop computer and search around. If you're creating Vegan shirts, for example, type in '#vegan.' You'll see at this moment #vegan has over 113 million posts. #veganlife has over 9.9 million, and #vegansofig has over 17 million. If you scroll down, you'll see more hashtags that are also relevant, like #vegancommunity, #veganlove, and #vegansofinstagram.

You can use this method for any hashtag or topic your brand is representing. Are you posting a shirt with an adorable dog? #dogmom, #dogdad, #doggo... search and see what other people are talking about, and be sure to include those hashtags!

The more you use popular hashtags that are relevant to your brand and your post, the more likely someone is to find your content organically. Be wary of using a hashtag that only has a few posts because it's clear that it's not a very popular choice. You can, however, have a brand hashtag.

If your company name Shirts By Kylie, for example, your hashtag could be #shirtsbykylie or #shirtsbyky, and you can use this hashtag on every post you make. Encourage your customers to share their photos wearing your product with your hashtag! You could even run competitions or offer giveaways for them tagging you – this is basically extremely cheap word-of-mouth advertising, and many people are more likely to buy from a new company if their friend or relative has vouched for them. Does that make sense to you?

If you find hashtags are cluttering up your posts, you can also drop your hashtags in the first comment. As with many things, I recommend you checking out the social media of some competitors just to get an idea of how they handle hashtags, what they choose, etc. Again, *do not* directly take their content; that is wrong on many levels.

However, you can gain inspiration and get a good baseline of what is working for other folks.

Do I Need TikTok?

Confession time: despite my experience advertising for my own brand, I didn't take TikTok seriously for a very long time. I thought it was a joke, it was a bad version of Vine, that it had no place in my marketing plan... basically, I saw it as a platform for 12-year-olds to connect with each other.

Yes, some of TikTok is that. But it has blown up in the past two years, and more people than ever are spending their evenings scrolling TikTok, watching funny videos, and finding new favorite brands.

In 2020, 32% of TikTok users were between 10-19 years of age. 29% are between 20-29, and 16.4% are between 30-29. The remaining 21% or so are 40+. These statistics surprise a lot of people who believed, as I did, that this is only a platform for kids.

TikTok can be difficult to advertise for some because it's

not a one-size-fits-all. Content on TikTok needs to be authentic! Users determine what becomes popular or not, and if it *feels* like intense advertising, they simply aren't going to accept it.

There are a few ways you can run ads on TikTok. **In-feed ads** are similar to Facebook and Instagram ads in that they show up in a user's general feed as they scroll through. You set the time, you set the market, and you let the advertisement do its thing. You should include a link to your shop within the post itself so that users can easily find your products.

This is the cheapest and easiest advertising on TikTok and the one I recommend utilizing, especially if you are just starting out. There are a few other choices, though — however, these are *very* expensive.

A **branded hashtag challenge** is something that is only found on TikTok, not other platforms. You can find hashtag challenges on the platforms Discovery page, which is where many users spend a lot of their time. When you click on a sponsored hashtag, you get a specific page with that brand.

A **branded lens** is also relatively common, and it is when your brand creates custom TikTok stickers, animations, and lenses for videos.

Brand Takeovers is a process where your advertisement takes up the whole screen when a user opens the app. It only allows one brand takeover per user per day, and this is *the most* expensive advertisement. I don't really recommend this, but it is an option for you. To give you perspective on cost, this starts at around $50,000 and goes up from there.

Similar to Instagram and Facebook, you can target your specific markets on TikTok as well. You can determine the gender, the age group, and even determine how active the folks you want to advertise to are.

The biggest thing to note is the difference between *Standard* delivery and *Accelerated* delivery. Standard delivery means that your entire budget will be distributed evenly throughout the time frame you have set, while accelerated delivery is going to blow through your budget faster to hit as many people as possible as quickly as possible.

Notes for Best Social Media Ad Practices

To reiterate, in order to get the most out of your social media accounts, be sure you:

Always start with a high-quality image, video, or post in general. Choose your best content that matches your brand and gets your point across.

Eye-catching video, music, and text are going to give you the best results.

Make it easy for the customer to follow through. That means always updating your link in bio or placing a link to your product or store within the post itself. If the viewer has to work to find your product, they are going to click away.

Don't be afraid to try new things and do a/b testing. Find out what works for your brand and for your target market!

Always pay attention to your results. If you're running a

campaign and it just didn't work out, put some thought into what went wrong. What is different from previous successful campaigns?

Don't let your ads run too long! Update your ads every week or so. If you run the same ad over and over again, your customers are going to be overexposed and generally uninterested by the end.

Connecting Your Social Media Accounts

I highly recommend that you connect all your business social media accounts! This will allow customers to easily find you on all platforms and keep your brand cohesive.

However, be wary of cross-posting on these platforms. It can be tempting to just make one post and shoot identical copies to all your other social media platforms, but that isn't really a great idea. If someone is following you on Instagram and Facebook, after all, they don't want to see the same post on both platforms.

It also makes your brand seem a little, well,

manufactured. It feels less like a real person and more like a robot making posts, and that really isn't a look you want! It takes a few extra minutes to customize each post for each platform, but it really is worth it in the long run.

Running Google Ads

Google Ads are the OG of the online advertising world. This is how people did it before social media became a big thing, and they are still used for a reason – it works! Depending on your target market, Google Ads could be just as effective as social media advertisements. Some folks aren't on social media or don't use it often enough for ads to really be effective.

Google Ads also offers a different way to target and advertise. Instead of focusing on your target market and showing only men aged 29-35 your ads, for example, Google Ads will target specific keywords. If someone is searching for *funny t-shirts, pet shirts, pun shirts, vegan shirts...* you get the drift. You can target these keywords and show anyone searching for these on your website.

You really only need a bare minimum of knowledge to get

started with Google Ads. I'm going to touch on the basics – if you want some serious in-depth knowledge, there are hours and hours of free tutorials on YouTube, but you really don't need that much information, especially just as you're starting.

Probably the most important thing to keep in mind is the **landing page** where your ad goes to. When a potential customer clicks on your advertisement, you want to be sure that they are going to a relevant page to the ad you ran and a page that is easy to read and navigate.

If your customers are clicking on an ad with a keyword about funny t-shirts, don't send them to an *About Us* page. They're immediately going to click away, and you're not going to see any benefit. Take them to a page that shows your best funny t-shirts!

Something a lot of people miss is thoroughly filling out the information, which is so silly, but it is missed! All add content and ad extensions should be up to date and properly filled out for the best results.

Finally, be careful with the way you choose keywords. Be

thoughtful with your keyword choices, don't just throw up an ad for 't-shirts' and call it a day. The more specific you get with your keywords, the better chance you have of finding someone looking for exactly what you're offering.

Select keywords that you believe your target market is searching for and keywords that fit *your* products. Try a Google search first to see how many results are showing up for your desired keywords and what sort of advertisements are running on them. That will give you an idea of just how specific you should be and what else is out there.

Other Marketing Options

Besides these major marketing opportunities, there are some things you can that help increase your exposure and bring in customers.

You can create a **blog** on your website to draw customers in and talk to them directly. You can discuss sales, upcoming events, your process in creating your shirts, and even just your life to generate interest.

If your target market is local, take advantage of local opportunities to sell and advertise. Dropping flyers or business cards at coffee shops and gathering places can catch the eye and bring interested folks to your site to learn more.

You should also spend time online where your target market hangs out! Answer questions on Quora, find communities on Reddit that align with your brand and your market to interact with, and post your products, as long as you're following the community guidelines. Build a reputation of a brand that people trust, and it's going to be absolutely worth the time and effort.

You should also always encourage your customers to leave reviews, post about your products, and start discussions online about that. Good word of mouth goes a *long way* to cultivating a brand and encouraging sales.

Speaking of Sales...

Not the same, but you might ask yourself: Should I have sales?

It's a question only you can answer, but you need to make sure whatever you put as a sale, you're still making a profit. You should never dip below that base price and lose money on your products.

However, sales are a great way to get new customers to pick up your products and generate interest. Seasonal sales are most common, especially during the holidays when everyone is buying for not just themselves, but others.

If you have a lot of products sitting around and you need to move it quickly, sales are always a good way to do so. Promote your sale with advertisements on social media, and doing a countdown to when the sale ends is a great way to build that immediate need to buy now without missing out.

Put It All Together, Now

So you know how to create your shirts. You know how you open a website and create a shop on that website to sell your products. You know marketing, you know social media, you understand the importance of creating an LLC...

I think you're ready to take the next steps. Do you think you're ready?

I'm not going to lie to you and tell you this journey is going to be very easy because it won't be. I've said it a hundred times, but if it's really worth doing, it's probably going to be hard. Your hard work, your drive, and your determination are what got to as far as you are, and it's what is going to take your business beyond just a hobby or a desire and to the next level.

I'm going to leave you with some points and reiterate the major things we have been over.

Choose a design type that fits your target market and

your life. Whether that's print on demand, bleach, or vinyl pressing, figure out what you enjoy doing *and* what your target market likes.

Speaking of target markets, determining your target market and then catering *to* that market is going to set you apart from all those other shops trying to just sell whatever to whoever. They will never reach the levels of success you are *able* to achieve if you only focus your view.

If you don't need it, don't buy it – at least, not right now. Don't overextend yourself or your business financially before you're off the ground. It's so tempting to buy the best and the nicest, but if you can get away with *not* doing it, you're going to put yourself ahead of the game. There is a time and place for splurging or buying the latest toys, and when you're starting on a budget? This isn't the time.

Take time to build your website, and make sure it is user-friendly. Would you be able to find products *you* like? You can even ask friends or family to check it over and get their honest feedback to help you grow and improve. You don't want your customers getting frustrated on your site and leaving before making a purchase!

Social media is your friend – do not hesitate to use it! You can promote products, share sales, and communicate with your customer base. Social media is the way of the future and of the now, and if you avoid using it, you're just missing out on major opportunities. So many small businesses neglect their social media accounts, and a little bit of polish and attention goes a long way to making yourself stand out.

Use the SMART system to create your goals, always. It works; it is taught in big business classes for a reason, so use it.

Create a business plan early, lay out goals for your business, and follow through. Keep a goal journal if that helps you, and every day mark how much farther you have gotten to reaching your goals and your dreams. It's important to mark the small wins and stay motivated and engaged. Otherwise, running a small business can feel like a lot of a grind without much reward.

In that vein, stay motivated and stay focused! You might get discouraged early on if you're not exploding in popularity right off the bat. You're going to get out what you put into it, but it can feel like a lot of work for not a lot of reward at first. Just keep your eyes on your goals and keep making progress towards them, and you can handle this.

Keep your business above board. Always pay your taxes, keep detailed receipts, and follow all federal, state, and even county regulations. It might seem like you can scoot around the laws, and no one will notice, but at some point, you'll run into a serious issue – and this can kill even the best businesses.

Price your products so that you *make* a profit and give your customers a price point they are comfortable with. Don't let customers bully you into discounts.

You can do this. You absolutely can start a business, sell the designs you love to any target market. When you feel stuck or frustrated, I encourage you to come back to this book. Read relevant chapters, ask yourself what you're doing differently or wrong, and figure out how to fix it.

I hope this guide was helpful to you, and you come away from it with more information than you started. The goal was a one-stop-shop for all your business needs and to get you to a place where you can immediately start your business and start making money *pronto*.

Keep your head up, your eyes on the prize – business ownership and success! – and keep pushing. There is no reason for you not to be able to be successful now.

Printed in Great Britain
by Amazon

35700821R00119